Vue.js 2 Design Patterns and Best Practices

Build enterprise-ready, modular Vue.js applications with Vuex and Nuxt

Paul Halliday

BIRMINGHAM - MUMBAI

D1361394

Vue.js 2 Design Patterns and Best Practices

Commissioning Editor: Kunal Chaudhari
Acquisition Editor: Shweta Pant
Content Development Editor: Flavian Vaz
Technical Editor: Diksha Wakode
Copy Editor: Safis Editing
Project Coordinator: Devanshi Doshi
Proofreader: Safis Editing
Indexer: Aishwarya Gangawane
Graphics: Jason Monteiro
Production Coordinator: Shraddha Falebhai

First published: March 2018

Production reference: 1080318

Published by Packt Publishing Ltd.
Livery Place
35 Livery Street
Birmingham
B3 2PB, UK.

ISBN 978-1-78883-979-2

www.packtpub.com

`mapt.io`

Mapt is an online digital library that gives you full access to over 5,000 books and videos, as well as industry leading tools to help you plan your personal development and advance your career. For more information, please visit our website.

Why subscribe?

- Spend less time learning and more time coding with practical eBooks and Videos from over 4,000 industry professionals

- Improve your learning with Skill Plans built especially for you

- Get a free eBook or video every month

- Mapt is fully searchable

- Copy and paste, print, and bookmark content

PacktPub.com

Did you know that Packt offers eBook versions of every book published, with PDF and ePub files available? You can upgrade to the eBook version at `www.PacktPub.com` and as a print book customer, you are entitled to a discount on the eBook copy. Get in touch with us at `service@packtpub.com` for more details.

At `www.PacktPub.com`, you can also read a collection of free technical articles, sign up for a range of free newsletters, and receive exclusive discounts and offers on Packt books and eBooks.

Contributors

About the author

Paul Halliday (BSc Hons) is a developer advocate with a focus on fast-moving technologies. His online courses have taught over 25,000 students across a wide variety of software development subjects. He's also a progress developer expert with expertize in NativeScript and Kendo UI.

About the reviewer

Pablo Henrique is a frontend developer, speaker, writer, and community leader focused on helping companies and individuals succeed with their frontend applications.
His current job as a Squad Leader at a Brazilian company gave him the opportunity to lead several developers' teams and to see the benefits of Vue.js while creating products and services.
He has given many presentations about Vue.js and has also reviewed *Vue.js 2.x by Example*, written by Mike Street.

> *I would like to thank my entire family for supporting me while doing this job, especially my mother (Flávia Penha de Freitas Silva) and my father (Ézio Walter da Silva). I would like to thank my girlfriend for having the patience and giving me insights while reviewing this book. I would like to thank Packt for this amazing opportunity.*

Packt is searching for authors like you

If you're interested in becoming an author for Packt, please visit `authors.packtpub.com` and apply today. We have worked with thousands of developers and tech professionals, just like you, to help them share their insight with the global tech community. You can make a general application, apply for a specific hot topic that we are recruiting an author for, or submit your own idea.

Table of Contents

Preface

Vue.js is a JavaScript framework that allows you to create performant web applications. It boasts a smaller learning curve than its competitors and has detailed documentation with a variety of examples and use cases. Vue.js applications can be created with the Vue CLI or by including it in your page via a `script` tag, making it super-easy to use in projects without build systems.

In a similar way to other modern web frameworks/libraries, Vue.js is component driven, and this means that you can create self-contained units with their own view/data logic. This allows our application to scale as it gets larger because any changes can be encapsulated away from each other.

When scaling your application, state management is a hot topic in the frontend space, and Vue.js solves this with the `Vuex` library. This allows us to define actions within our application and act accordingly, giving us predictable state that can be used to form the basis of our user interface and other interactions.

This book explores all this and more, and it provides examples of how these principles can be implemented into new and old Vue.js applications.

Who this book is for

This book is for people interested in creating web and mobile applications with JavaScript. Prior experience with HTML5/ES2015 will be helpful, as modern JavaScript concepts are used within the book. You'll likely be looking to make use of this knowledge to create interactive web-based experiences within your personal projects or job role.

What this book covers

Chapter 1, *Vue.js Principles and Comparisons*, introduces the readers to Vue.js and motivates them to use it as a framework to create web applications. The reader will gain an understanding of the differences between Vue.js in comparison to other popular frameworks, such as React and Angular.

Chapter 2, *Proper Creation of Vue Projects*, looks at the appropriate way to create a Vue project. This includes the use of Webpack, Babel/TypeScript (for ES6), `.vue` files, linting, and more.

Chapter 3, *Writing Clean and Lean Code with Vue*, takes a deeper look at the Vue.js instance and different reserved properties, such as data, computed, and watch, as well as creating getters and setters. This chapter especially considers when to use computed properties and when to use watched properties. It also outlines why templates should be kept especially lean for easier maintenance.

Chapter 4, *Vue.js Directives*, introduces the fact that the developers have access to a powerful set of directives, such as v-for, v-if, v-model, and others when writing reactive Vue applications. This chapter looks at each directive in detail, as well as best practices and patterns. Furthermore, the reader is introduced to using shorthand syntax for event binding.

Chapter 5, *Secured Communication with Vue.js Components*, takes a more advanced look at Vue components, with a look at component communication. We'll take a look at passing properties, as well as validating for prop types and considering the different types of properties and data flows.

Chapter 6, *Creating Better UI*, focuses on the common UI patterns of Vue. It takes another look at how v-model can be used to gain input from the user, along with a glance at binding to inputs such as text, checkbox, radio buttons, and so on. It also looks at drop-down and dynamic inputs. Finally, the chapter covers form submission and various modifiers, such as lazy binding, number typecasting, and string trimming.

Chapter 7, *HTTP and WebSocket Communication*, covers the best practices for integrating HTTP into Vue.js applications. It takes a look at Axios and a variety of methods for sending HTTP requests (that is, root instance/component/ nav guards). This chapter also takes a look at using socket.io, along with the creation of a basic Node/ Express API for real-time integration.

Chapter 8, *Vue Router Patterns*, describes how routing is a vitally important part of any SPA. This chapter focuses on the Vue route and looks at routing a user between multiple pages. It goes through everything from matching paths and components to dynamic matching with navigation parameters, regular expressions, and more.

Chapter 9, *State Management with Vuex*, demonstrates state management with Vuex. It starts by looking at the Flux architecture and unidirectional data flow. Then, it takes a look at Vuex, a state management system for Vue. The chapter also looks at implementing this in an application, as well as common pitfalls and usage patterns. It goes on to the Vue-devtools to capture actions and Vue instance data.

Chapter 10, *Testing Vue.js Applications*, demonstrates that testing is a vital part of any project, regardless of the framework or language. This chapter looks at testing our application and how to write testable code. We'll then look at testing our application with Jasmine and Karma, as well as testing our Vuex code when testing mutations.

Chapter 11, *Optimization*, outlines deploying a Vue application and any potential performance optimizations. It then looks at converting an application to a **Progressive Web App (PWA)** and adding ServiceWorkers, offline support, and more. It also looks at ways in which the overall bundle size can be reduced, and at performance wins with SVG.

Chapter 12, *Server-Side Rendering with Nuxt*, showcases using Nuxt to create Vue applications that are server-side rendered. The project will be created by using the Vue CLI, and we'll look at everything from configuration to routing, middleware, and testing Nuxt, all the way through to deployment.

Chapter 13, *Patterns*, assists the reader with common anti-patterns and allows them to avoid these principles when writing Vue.js applications. A style guide is proposed, as well as key issues such as the use of $parent, $ref coupling issues, inline expressions, and others.

To get the most out of this book

1. You should already have an understanding and knowledge of JavaScript (ES2015+), as well as HTML5 and CSS3.
2. Experience with Vue.js is not required for this book, although experience with other JavaScript frameworks will assist with comparisons and similar features.

Download the example code files

You can download the example code files for this book from your account at www.packtpub.com. If you purchased this book elsewhere, you can visit www.packtpub.com/support and register to have the files emailed directly to you.

You can download the code files by following these steps:

1. Log in or register at www.packtpub.com.
2. Select the **SUPPORT** tab.

3. Click on **Code Downloads & Errata**.
4. Enter the name of the book in the **Search** box and follow the onscreen instructions.

Once the file is downloaded, please make sure that you unzip or extract the folder using the latest version of:

- WinRAR/7-Zip for Windows
- Zipeg/iZip/UnRarX for Mac
- 7-Zip/PeaZip for Linux

The code bundle for the book is also hosted on GitHub at https://github.com/ PacktPublishing/Vue.js-2-Design-Patterns-and-Best-Practices.

We also have other code bundles from our rich catalog of books and videos available at https://github.com/PacktPublishing/. Check them out!

Download the color images

We also provide a PDF file that has color images of the screenshots/diagrams used in this book. You can download it here: https://www.packtpub.com/sites/default/files/ downloads/Vuejs2DesignPatternsandBestPractices_ColorImages.pdf.

Conventions used

There are a number of text conventions used throughout this book.

CodeInText: Indicates code words in the text, database table names, folder names, filenames, file extensions, pathnames, dummy URLs, user input, and Twitter handles. Here is an example: "Mount the downloaded WebStorm-10*.dmg disk image file as another disk in your system."

A block of code is set as follows:

```
// my-module.js
export default function add(x, y) {
  return x + y
}
```

Any command-line input or output is written as follows:

```
$ npm install
$ npm run dev
```

Bold: Indicates a new term, an important word, or words that you see onscreen. For example, words in menus or dialog boxes appear in the text like this. Here is an example: "Select **System info** from the **Administration** panel."

 Warnings or important notes appear like this.

 Tips and tricks appear like this.

Get in touch

Feedback from our readers is always welcome.

General feedback: Email `feedback@packtpub.com` and mention the book title in the subject of your message. If you have questions about any aspect of this book, please email us at `questions@packtpub.com`.

Errata: Although we have taken every care to ensure the accuracy of our content, mistakes do happen. If you have found a mistake in this book, we would be grateful if you would report this to us. Please visit `www.packtpub.com/submit-errata`, selecting your book, clicking on the Errata Submission Form link, and entering the details.

Piracy: If you come across any illegal copies of our works in any form on the Internet, we would be grateful if you would provide us with the location address or website name. Please contact us at `copyright@packtpub.com` with a link to the material.

If you are interested in becoming an author: If there is a topic that you have expertise in and you are interested in either writing or contributing to a book, please visit `authors.packtpub.com`.

Reviews

Please leave a review. Once you have read and used this book, why not leave a review on the site that you purchased it from? Potential readers can then see and use your unbiased opinion to make purchase decisions, we at Packt can understand what you think about our products, and our authors can see your feedback on their book. Thank you!

For more information about Packt, please visit `packtpub.com`.

1
Vue.js Principles and Comparisons

In this chapter, we'll be looking at why Vue is an important web development framework, as well as looking at setting up our development environment. If we're looking to use Vue for our next project, it's important we realize the implications, time investment, and learning curve when doing so. You'll have considered how Vue shapes up to other frontend development projects, as well as creating your first application with Vue.

In summary, we'll be considering the following points:

- Downloading the book prerequisites
- Understanding of where Vue fits into a frontend framework
- Why you should consider using Vue as the framework for your next project
- Investigation of how flexible Vue is and its role in mobile development

Prerequisites

Although you could develop Vue applications without Node, we'll be using Node.js throughout this book to manage dependencies and interact with the Vue **Command Line Interface (CLI)**. This allows us to bootstrap projects quicker and gives us a better development experience as we can use ECMAScript 2015 by default. Let's have a quick refresher on setting up your development environment.

Windows

Installing Node for Windows is as simple as visiting `https://nodejs.org` and downloading the latest version. Ensure that when following the installation steps, **Add to PATH** is selected as this will allow us to access node commands within our Terminal.

Once you've done that, check your Node installation works by typing `node -v` and `npm -v`. If you get two version numbers back (that is, one for each), then you're ready to go ahead with the rest of the book!

Mac

Installing Node for Mac involves a little more work than simply downloading the installer from the Node website. While it is possible to use the installer from `https://nodejs.org`, it is not advised due to the requirement of `sudo`.

If we did it this way, we'd have to prefix all of our `npm` commands with `sudo` and this can leave our system vulnerable to potential scripting attacks and is inconvenient. Instead, we can install Node via the Homebrew package manager and we can then interact with `npm` without worrying about having to run things as `sudo`.

Another great thing about using Homebrew to install Node is that it's automatically added to our PATH. This means we'll be able to type node commands without having to fiddle around with our environment files.

Installing Node via Homebrew

The quickest way to get Homebrew is to visit `http://brew.sh` and get hold of the installation script. It should look a little something like this:

```
/usr/bin/ruby -e "$(curl -fsSL
https://raw.githubusercontent.com/Homebrew/install/master/install)"
```

Simply paste that into your Terminal and it'll download the Homebrew package manager to your Mac. We can then use brew install node to install Node on our system without any worries.

Once you've done that, check your Node installation works by typing `node -v` and `npm -v`. If you get two version numbers back (that is, one for each), then you're ready to go ahead with the rest of the book!

In order to manage the different Node versions, we could also install the **Node Version Manager (NVM)**. Do note however that this is currently only supported by Mac at present and not Windows. To install NVM, we can use Homebrew like so:

```
--use Brew to install the NVM
brew install nvm

--File directory
mkdir ~/.nvm

--Install latest version
nvm install --lts

--Ensure latest version is used
nvm use node

--Remember details across sessions
nano ~/.bash_profile

--Execute in every session
export NVM_DIR="$HOME/.nvm"
  . "$(brew --prefix nvm)/nvm.sh"
```

Editor

A variety of editors can be used, such as Visual Studio Code, Sublime Text, Atom, and WebStorm. I recommend Visual Studio Code (https://code.visualstudio.com) as it has a frequent release cycle and a wealth of Vue extensions that we can use to improve our workflow.

Browser

We will be using Google Chrome to run our project(s) as this has an extension named Vue devtools that is instrumental to our development workflow. If you do not use Google Chrome, ensure your browser has the same Vue devtools extension that is available for usage.

Installing the Vue devtools

Head over to the Google Chrome Extensions store and download Vue.js devtools (`https://goo.gl/Sc3YU1`). After installing this, you'll then have access to the Vue panel within your developer tools. In the following example, we're able to see the data object inside of our Vue instance:

```html
<!DOCTYPE html>
<html lang="en">
<head>
  <meta charset="UTF-8">
  <meta name="viewport" content="width=device-width, initial-scale=1.0">
  <meta http-equiv="X-UA-Compatible" content="ie=edge">
  <title>Vue.js</title>
</head>
<body>
  <div id="app"></div>
  <script src="http://unpkg.com/vue"></script>
  <script>
   Vue.config.devtools = true
   new Vue({
     el: '#app',
     data: {
       name: 'Vue.js Devtools',
       browser: 'Google Chrome'
     },
     template: `
      <div>
        <h1> I'm using {{name}} with {{browser}}</h1>
      </div>
      `
   });
  </script>
</body>
</html>
```

If we then head over to our browser and open up the devtools we can see that Vue has been detected and that our message has outputted on to the screen:

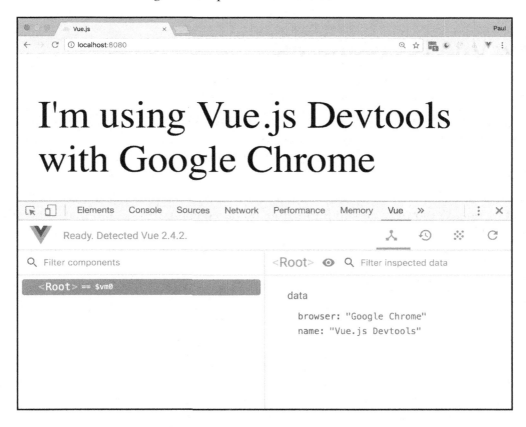

We'll be using this throughout the book to gain extra insight into our applications. Do be aware that the developer tools will only recognize your Vue project if it is served on a local server.

Vue CLI

To take advantage of all of the features of Vue, we'll be using Vue CLI. This allows us to create projects with various starter templates with appropriate bundling/transpilation configurations. Type the following into your Terminal ensuring Node is installed:

```
$ npm install vue-cli -g
```

This sets us up for the future sections as using starter templates significantly empowers our workflow.

How Vue.js compares

This book seeks to outline how to best structure your Vue applications with common development patterns, best practices, and anti-patterns to avoid.

Our journey starts by taking a look at how Vue shapes up to other common projects, and if you measure your frameworks by GitHub stars, Vue is clearly a future winner. According to `https://bestof.js.org`, in 2017 it currently measures at 114 stars per day in comparison to React's 76 and Angular's 32.

Framework discussion when talking about modern web development technologies is an interesting one. Very rarely do you find a true, unbiased comparison... but that's fine! It's not about which framework or library is best, but rather what's best for your team, project goals, consumers, and hundreds of other variables. As a Vue developer, you're likely a person that wants to build reactive web applications with a simple, easy-to-use API.

It's this adaptable, easy-to-use API that makes Vue pleasant to work with, and perhaps one of the strongest points of Vue is the simple, focused documentation. It has a significantly low barrier to entry: simply add a script file from a CDN, initialize a new Vue instance... and you're away! Granted, there's much more to Vue than this, but in contrast to some fully fledged frameworks such as Angular, you'd be forgiven for thinking it's that easy.

Vue uses templates, declarative bindings, and a component-based architecture to separate concerns and make projects easier to maintain. This becomes especially important when considering which framework to use inside of an enterprise. Usually, this is where projects such Angular shine as it's ability to enforce standards across the entire project.

We've established it's easy to use, but Vue is quite young in comparison to its competitors... how do we know it's not all hype? Is it being used in production by anyone? It certainly is! GitLab recently wrote an article about why they chose Vue.js (`https://about.gitlab.com/2016/10/20/why-we-chose-vue/`), and the primary benefits they cited were ease of use, less code, and fewer assumptions. Other companies such as Laravel, Nintendo, Sainsbury's and Alibaba are all following this route and even companies such as Rever Shine rewrote their web client from Angular 2.x to Vue 2.x (`https://medium.com/reverdev/why-we-moved-from-angular-2-to-vue-js-and-why-we-didnt-choose-react-ef807d9f4163`).

It's not just public – facing web applications that are taking advantage of Vue.js—NativeScript Sidekick (`https://www.nativescript.org/blog/announcing-the-nativescript-sidekick-public-preview`), a project focused on improving the NativeScript development experience, is built with Electron and Vue.js.

If we gain some insights from the State of JavaScript survey (`http://2016.stateofjs.com/2016/frontend/`) by Sacha Greif (`https://twitter.com/SachaGreif`) and Michael Rambeau (`http://michaelrambeau.com/`), we can see that a whopping **89%** of people used Vue before and want to use it again. Other libraries such as React have similar satisfaction rates at **92%**, but Angular 2 and onwards didn't see anywhere near as much love, with **65%** wanting to use it again:

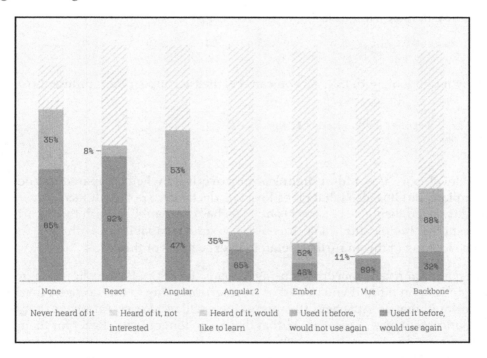

What other options are available to us as frontend developers? How do they shape up to Vue? Let's start with React.

React

React is a JavaScript library developed and maintained by Facebook, and is largely the closest comparison to Vue as their goals are very similar. Like Vue, React is component based and takes advantage of Virtual DOM concepts. This allows for performant rendering of DOM nodes, as a different algorithm is used to determine which parts of the DOM have changed and how best to render/update them on change.

When it comes to templates, React uses JSX to render items on the screen. It takes the more verbose way of creating DOM elements with `React.createElement` and simplifies it like so:

This is how it will look without JSX:

```
React.createElement</span>( MyButton, {color: 'red', shadowSize: 5}, 'Click
Me' )
```

Here is how it will look with JSX. As you can see, the two appear very different from one another:

```
<MyButton color="red" shadowSize={5}>
  Click Me
</MyButton>
```

For newer developers, this adds a slight learning overhead when compared to Vue's simple HTML template, but it is also what gives React its declarative power. It has a state management system using `setState()`, but also has compatibility with third-party state containers such as Redux and MobX. Vue also has similar capabilities with the `Vuex` library, and we'll be looking at this in further detail in later sections of this book.

One of the common recent concerns of using React is the BSD + Patents license agreement, something to keep in mind if you're part of an enterprise. Due to this license, Apache recently declared that no Apache software products will use React. Another example of this is the announcement by `Wordpress.com` that they're no longer using React for their Gutenberg project (`https://ma.tt/2017/09/on-react-and-wordpress/`). This doesn't necessarily mean that you shouldn't use React in your projects, but is worth pointing out nonetheless.

Some concerned developers elect to use alternatives such as Preact but more recently Vue.js, as it meets a lot of the goals that React developers are looking for when developing applications. To that end, Microsoft (`http://dev.office.com/fabric#/components`), Apple (`https://developer.apple.com/documentation`), and countless other companies have products released with React – make of that what you will.

Angular

Angular is an opinionated JavaScript framework developed and maintained by Google. At the time of writing, it's currently approaching version 5 and offers a structured standards-based approach to web development. It uses TypeScript to enforce type safety and ECMAScript 2015 > support.

In comparison to Angular, Vue looks to enforce a smaller set of constraints and allows the developer more choice. One of Angular's core competencies is TypeScript everywhere. Most developers that came from Angular.js were hearing about TypeScript for the first time when Angular 2 was announced, and I noticed a fair amount of backlash because of the need to "learn a new language". The thing is, JavaScript is TypeScript and the value of increased tooling (autocompletion, refactoring, type safety, and much more) cannot be overlooked.

This is especially true when it comes to working on enterprise projects as the onboarding challenge gets harder with increased project complexity and team size. With TypeScript, we're able to better reason about the relationships between our code at scale. It's this structured development experience that is the prime strength of Angular. This is why the Angular team chose TypeScript as the primary development tool. The benefits of TypeScript are not limited to Angular; we'll be looking at how we can integrate Vue with TypeScript to gain these same benefits later on in the book.

Are there any drawbacks to using Angular as a development framework? Not necessarily. When we're comparing it to Vue, the onboarding experience is vitally different.

Mobile development

When it comes to developing mobile applications, projects such as Angular and React are great choices for developing mobile-first applications. The success of the NativeScript, React Native, and Ionic Framework projects have boosted the significant popularity of these frameworks. For instance, Ionic Framework currently has more stars than Angular on GitHub!

Vue is making waves in this area with projects such as NativeScript Vue, Weex, and Quasar Framework. All of the listed projects are relatively new, but it only takes one to truly spike the popularity of Vue in production even further. Using NativeScript Vue as an example, it only takes 43 lines of code to create a cross-platform mobile application that connects to a REST API and displays the results on screen. If you'd like to follow along with this yourself, run:

```
# Install the NativeScript CLI
npm install nativescript -g
```

```
# New NativeScript Vue project
tns create NSVue --template nativescript-vue-template

# Change directory
cd NSVue

# Run on iOS
tns run ios
```

Then, we can place the following inside of our app/app.js:

```
const Vue = require('nativescript-vue/dist/index');
const http = require('http');
Vue.prototype.$http = http;

new Vue({
    template: `
    <page>
        <action-bar class="action-bar" title="Posts"></action-bar>
        <stack-layout>
            <list-view :items="posts">
                <template scope="post">
                    <stack-layout class="list">
                        <label :text="post.title"></label>
                        <label :text="post.body"></label>
                    </stack-layout>
                </template>
            </list-view>
        </stack-layout>
    </page>
    `,
    data: {
        posts: []
    },
    created(args) {
        this.getPosts();
    },
    methods: {
        getPosts() {
            this.$http
                .getJSON(`https://jsonplaceholder.typicode.com/posts`)
                .then(response => {
                    this.posts = response.map(
                        post => {
                            return {
                                title: post.title,
                                body: post.body
                            }
```

```
                    }
                  )
                });
              }
            }
          }).$start();
```

If we then run our code, we can see a list of posts. You'll notice that our Vue code is declarative, and we have the power of larger frameworks at our disposal with much less code:

Server-Side Rendering (SSR)

Server-Side Rendering allows us to take our frontend JavaScript application and render it to static HTML on the server. This is important as it allows us to significantly speed up our application as the browser only has to parse the critical HTML/CSS. Maximizing performance is a key component of modern day web applications and the expectation continues to grow with progressive web applications and projects such as AMP. Both React, Angular and Vue are capable of SSR using a variety of different patterns.

Let's take a look at how we can achieve a simple Server-Side rendered Vue application:

```
# Create a new folder named vue-ssr:
$ mkdir vue-ssr
$ cd vue-ssr

# Create a new file named server.js
$ touch server.js

# Install dependencies
$ npm install vue vue-server-renderer express
```

Inside `server.js`, we can create a new Vue instance and use the Vue renderer to output the content of our instance as an HTML:

```
const Vue = require("vue");
const server = require("express")();
const renderer = require("vue-server-renderer").createRenderer();

server.get("*", (req, res) => {
  const app = new Vue({
    data: {
      date: new Date()
    },
    template: `
    <div>
    The visited time: {{ date }}
    </div>`
  });

  renderer.renderToString(app, (err, html) => {
    if (err) {
      res.status(500).end("Internal Server Error");
      return;
    }
    res.end(`
      <!DOCTYPE html>
```

```
    <html lang="en">
      <head><title>Hello</title></head>
      <body>${html}</body>
    </html>
    `);
  });
});

server.listen(8080);
```

To run the application, type the following in the Terminal:

```
$ node server.js
```

We can then open this in our browser at `http://localhost: 8080` and we'd see the current date and time on screen. This is a simple example but we were able to see our application rendered using the `vue-server-renderer`. Notice how we're not defining a target element to render content within our Vue instance; this is handled by the `renderer.renderToString` function.

You'll also notice that we have the `data-server-rendered="true"` attribute on our DOM node, which isn't present on a client-side rendered Vue application. This allows us to hydrate our client-side instance with our server-side instance, something we'll be looking at more detail in the later chapter(s) on Nuxt (`https://nuxtjs.org/`).

Conclusion

The choice of web framework in the enterprise is always going to be dependent on the goals of your project, team, and organizational priorities. No one framework is the correct choice, because optimal means different things depending on the context. Each framework or library has its own unique benefits, drawbacks, and priorities. If your priority is to create web applications quickly and at scale, Vue can compete with the other market solutions.

Vue is feature rich, declarative, and highly legible. Even though it's a simplistic framework, the declarative nature of Vue allows us to get up and running at blazing fast speed without having to worry about overly complex patterns.

Summary

In this chapter, we looked at how we can set up our development environment and how Vue is being used in many products throughout the industry. We've learned that Vue is a simple, yet powerful frontend development framework. As well as this, we've considered how Vue shapes up when compared to other popular projects, such as Angular and React. We've also looked at how Vue works with other technologies, such as NativeScript, to create cross-platform native mobile applications. Finally, we've investigated SSR at a high level and set the stage for chapters to come. Hopefully, by now you're convinced that Vue is worth learning, and you're looking forward to taking advantage of all it has to offer!

In the next chapter, we'll be looking at the Vue CLI and how to take advantage of tools such as Webpack to create our Vue projects. As well as this, we'll look at how to take advantage of static types and tooling with TypeScript and reactive observable patterns with RxJS within Vue.

2
Proper Creation of Vue Projects

In this chapter, we'll be looking at how we can create maintainable Vue projects, and take advantage of the many tools and patterns available. If you currently aren't maximizing the use of these things within your development workflow, you may find that the majority of the concepts we discuss in this chapter are applicable to other technologies.

In this chapter, we will be looking at the following:

- Vue devtools
- Visual Studio Code extensions
- TypeScript integration
- Reactivity with RxJS

Visual Studio Code extensions

Our development environment is an important part of application development. When using Visual Studio Code to create Vue applications, the following extensions are recommended:

- Vetur
- Vue 2 Snippets

Let's take a look at both of these in more detail.

Vetur

Vetur is powered by the Vue Language Server and provides us with syntax highlighting, Emmet (for increased HTML/CSS workflow), snippets, linting, IntelliSense, and more. This greatly improves our development experience and is widely supported, with over 1,000 stars on GitHub. To install the extension, click the **Extensions** icon within Visual Studio Code and type Vetur; from here, you can select **Install** and it'll automatically be used throughout your project(s):

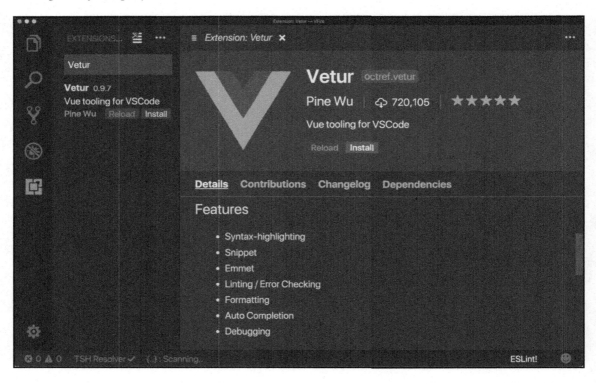

Installing Vetur

This then gives us access to snippets such as `scaffold`, which generates a new blank template, script, and style object(s) for us to use within our Vue components:

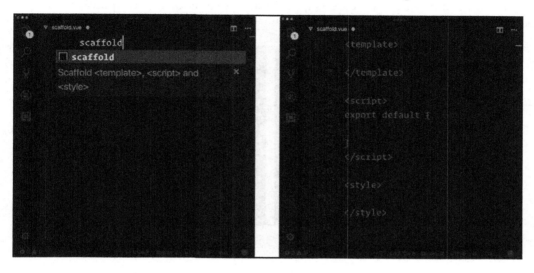

Scaffolding a new Vue project

Vue 2 Snippets

Snippets are an important part of application development; in a similar way to Emmet, they allow us to quickly scaffold common patterns within our application. We'll also be installing another Visual Studio Code extension that provides us with a variety of commonly used snippets named Vue 2 Snippets.

This allows us to save a substantial amount of time that we otherwise would have had to spend writing out the same boilerplate code. Take the next example; although it's simplistic in nature, we get a description of the snippet, and with a hit of *Tab* it expands to our predefined code:

Taking advantage of Vue snippets

Vue CLI

The Vue **Command Line Interface** (**CLI**) allows us to quickly scaffold new Vue projects with a variety of different template options. Currently, the template options available include technologies such as Webpack, Browserify, and Progressive Web Application features.

Sure, we could create our own Vue application and manually add tools such as Webpack, but this creates technical overhead in the sense that we have to learn, build, and maintain our configuration. The Vue CLI does this for us while maintaining a select set of official templates, but doesn't restrict us from modifying the generated Webpack configuration. All of this allows us to generate new unopinionated Vue projects.

To start using the Vue CLI, let's ensure we have it installed:

```
npm install vue-cli -g
```

We can then use the Vue `init` command to scaffold a new Vue project using the Webpack template:

```
vue init webpack-simple my-vue-project
```

On entering the preceding command we should get the following as shown on the Terminal:

```
Pauls-MBP:repos paulhalliday$ vue init webpack-simple my-vue-proj
ect

? Project name my-vue-project
? Project description A Vue.js project
? Author Paul Halliday
? Use sass? No

  vue-cli · Generated "my-vue-project".

  To get started:

    cd my-vue-project
    npm install
    npm run dev.

Pauls-MBP:repos paulhalliday$ ▌
```

Creating projects with Vue init

If we break this down, we're essentially initializing a new Vue project based on the **webpack-simple** template named **my-vue-project**. We're then navigated to a wizard process that asks us for more metadata about our project. This metadata and configuration will differ depending on the template you choose.

Let's investigate the files and folders that the template created:

File/Folder	Description
src/	This folder contains all of our project code. We'll spend the majority of our time within src.
.bablrc	This is our Babel configuration file that allows us to write ES2015 and have it appropriately transpiled.
index.html	This is our default HTML file.
package.json	This holds our dependencies and other project-specific metadata.
webpack.config.js	This is our Webpack configuration file, allowing us to use .vue files, Babel, and more.

Notice how we're no longer working with `.js` files, and we now have `.vue` files inside of our `src` directory. A Vue file is known as a Single File Component and it has a template, script, and style tag, allowing us to scope everything to this component only.

This is possible due to our Webpack template, as we have a custom "loader". How does this work? Prior to looking at this, let's take a quick detour and review modern JavaScript build systems.

JavaScript modules

In order to create reusable modular code, our aim should be to have one file per feature in most cases. This allows us to avoid the dreaded "Spaghetti code" anti-pattern, where we have strong coupling and little separation of concerns. Continuing with the pasta-oriented theme, the solution to this is to embrace the "Ravioli code" pattern with smaller, loosely coupled, distributed modules that are easier to work with. What does a JavaScript module look like?

In ECMAScript2015, a module is simply a file that uses the `export` keyword, and allows other modules to then import that piece of functionality:

```
// my-module.js
export default function add(x, y) {
  return x + y
}
```

We could then `import add` from another module:

```
// my-other-module.js
import { add } from './my-other-module'

add(1, 2) // 3
```

As browsers haven't fully caught up with module imports yet, we often use tools to assist with the bundling process. Common projects in this area are Babel, Bublé, Webpack, and Browserify. When we create a new project with the Webpack template, it uses the Vue-loader to transform our Vue components into a standard JavaScript module.

Vue-loader

Inside of our `./webpack-config.js` within the standard `webpack-simple` template, we have a module object that allows us to set up our loader; this tells Webpack that we'd like it to use `.vue` files inside of our project:

```
module: {
 rules: [{
  test: /\.vue$/,
  loader: 'vue-loader',
  options: {
   loaders: {}
  // other vue-loader options go here
  }
 }]
```

For this to work, Webpack runs a regular expression for anything that matches `.vue` and then passes this to our `vue-loader` to be transformed into a plain JavaScript module. In this simple example, we're loading files with a `.vue` extension, but `vue-loader` can be further customized and you may want to look into this further (`https://goo.gl/4snNfD`). We could certainly do this configuration ourselves, but hopefully, you can see the benefits of using the Vue CLI to generate our Webpack projects.

Loading modules without Webpack

Although Webpack helps us in more ways than simply loading a module, we can load a JavaScript module at this moment in time natively in the browser. It tends to perform worse than bundling tools (at the time of writing), but this may change over time.

To demonstrate this, let's head over to the terminal and make a simple counter with a project based on the simple template. This template effectively starts a new Vue project without any bundling tools:

```
# New Vue Project
vue init simple vue-modules

# Navigate to Directory
cd vue-modules

# Create App and Counter file
touch app.js
touch counter.js
```

We can then edit our `index.html` to add script files from `type="module"` this allows us to use the export/import syntax outlined before:

```html
<!-- index.html -->
<!DOCTYPE html>
<html>
<head>
 <title>Vue.js Modules - Counter</title>
 <script src="https://unpkg.com/vue"></script>
</head>
<body>
 <div id="app">
 </div>
 <script type="module" src="counter.js"></script>
 <script type="module" src="app/app.js"></script>
</body>
</html>
```

Warning: Ensure that your browser is up to date so that the preceding code can run successfully.

Then, inside of our `counter.js`, we can export a new `default` object, which acts as a new Vue instance. It acts as a simple counter that allows us to either increment or decrements a value:

```js
export default {
 template: `
  <div>
   <h1>Counter: {{counter}}</h1>
   <button @click="increment">Increment</button>
   <button @click="decrement">Decrement</button>
  </div>`,
 data() {
  return {
   counter: 1
  };
 },
 methods: {
  increment() {
   this.counter++;
  },
  decrement() {
   this.counter--;
```

```
    }
  }
};
```

We can then import the `counter.js` file inside of `app.js`, thus demonstrating the ways we can import/export modules. To get our counter to display inside of our root Vue instance, we're registering the counter as a component inside this instance, and setting the template to `<counter></counter>`, the name of our component:

```
import Counter from './counter.js';

const app = new Vue({
  el: '#app',
  components: {
    Counter
  },
  template: `<counter></counter>`
});
```

We'll look at this in more detail in future sections of the book, but all you need to know at this point is that it effectively acts as another Vue instance. When we register the component inside of our instance, we're only able to access this component from that instance.

Awesome! Here are the results of our module import/exports:

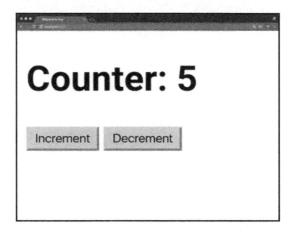

Vue.js Modules

In the next section, we'll take a deeper look at debugging our Vue applications, and the role Vue devtools plays in this.

VueJS devtools

Being able to accurately debug our application is an important part of our development workflow. In the previous chapter, we installed the VueJS devtools, and we'll be looking at using it in more detail within this section. Let's make a playground project:

```
# New project
vue init webpack-simple vue-devtools

# Change directory
cd vue-devtools

# Install dependencies
npm install

# Run application
npm run dev
```

We can then open up our developer console and navigate to the **Vue** tab. When we select **App** from within the components list, we can see the data object(s) and other information for this component. By default, we have the msg variable that we're then binding to within our template, and we can see this within our developer tools:

Inspecting a Vue instance

This goes both ways though - we could access the objects inside of this Vue instance with `$vm0.$data`, scoping this to `msg`. To view this within the console, selecting `<Root>` then `<App>` will display the `msg0;`within the console. We can change this value and as Vue is watching the value, it will automatically change on screen:

Editing Vue instance data from the console

Notice how our message has changed to `"Hello Vue Devtools!"`; if we had multiple Vue instances, there would be other prefixed versions of Vue with `$vm1`, `$vm2`, and so on. Later in the book when we come to using `Vuex`, we'll be using this often. Next, let's take a look at how we can integrate TypeScript into our Vue projects. This is useful for those with an Angular background or anyone that's looking to take advantage of static typing.

TypeScript and Vue

You may have used TypeScript in the past, or you may be curious about how you can take advantage of the extra tooling TypeScript provides inside of your Vue projects. Why use TypeScript? A recent study by Gao et al found that TypeScript/static typing tools reduced committed bugs by 15% (https://goo.gl/XUTPf4).

If you've used Angular before, this syntax should make you feel right at home, as we'll be using decorators and ES2015 classes. Let's investigate how we can add TypeScript to a project built with the Vue CLI:

```
# Create a new Vue project
vue init webpack-simple typescript-vue

# Change directory
cd typescript-vue

# Install dependencies
npm install
```

You should get the following output on the Terminal:

```
Pauls-MBP:repos paulhalliday$ vue init webpack-simple typescript-vue

? Project name typescript-vue
? Project description Integrating TypeScript and Vue
? Author Paul Halliday
? Use sass? No

   vue-cli · Generated "typescript-vue".

   To get started:

     cd typescript-vue
     npm install
     npm run dev.

Pauls-MBP:repos paulhalliday$
```

If we navigate to our project directory and run `npm install` as per the instructions, we then need to install the TypeScript loader and edit our Webpack configuration. This allows us to load `.ts` files inside of the project, and because we've used the `webpack-simple` template, it's as simple as installing the loader and making a few changes. At the same time, we can also install TypeScript to the project:

```
# Install TypeScript and the TypeScript Loader
npm install typescript ts-loader --save-dev
```

We then need to make some changes to our Webpack configuration to add our new loader. Hot Module Replacement is enabled by default, so there is no need to refresh to see any changes once loaded.

 Remember to run the project from the command line, and type `npm dev`.

We need to change our entry point to be `main.ts` (and subsequently rename it), as well as define the `ts-loader` and remove the `babel-loader` in order to do it, and edit the `webpack.config.js` file, pasting the following contents:

```
var path = require('path');
var webpack = require('webpack');

module.exports = {
  entry: './src/main.ts',
  output: {
  path: path.resolve(__dirname, './dist'),
  publicPath: '/dist/',
  filename: 'build.js'
  },
  module: {
  rules: [
  {
  test: /\.vue$/,
  loader: 'vue-loader',
  options: {
  loaders: {}
  }
  },
  {
  test: /\.tsx?$/,
  loader: 'ts-loader',
  exclude: /node_modules/,
  options: {
```

```
appendTsSuffixTo: [/\.vue$/]
}
},
{
test: /\.(png|jpg|gif|svg)$/,
loader: 'file-loader',
options: {
name: '[name].[ext]?[hash]'
}
}
]
},
resolve: {
extensions: ['.ts', '.js', '.vue'],
alias: {
vue$: 'vue/dist/vue.esm.js'
}
},
devServer: {
historyApiFallback: true,
noInfo: true
},
performance: {
hints: false
},
devtool: '#eval-source-map'
};

if (process.env.NODE_ENV === 'production') {
module.exports.devtool = '#source-map';
// http://vue-loader.vuejs.org/en/workflow/production.html
module.exports.plugins = (module.exports.plugins || []).concat([
new webpack.DefinePlugin({
'process.env': {
NODE_ENV: '"production"'
}
}),
new webpack.optimize.UglifyJsPlugin({
sourceMap: true,
compress: {
warnings: false
}
}),
new webpack.LoaderOptionsPlugin({
minimize: true
})
]);
}
```

After this, we can create a `tsconfig.json` inside of our project root, which is responsible for appropriately configuring our TypeScript setup:

```
{
  "compilerOptions": {
  "lib": ["dom", "es5", "es2015"],
  "module": "es2015",
  "target": "es5",
  "moduleResolution": "node",
  "experimentalDecorators": true,
  "sourceMap": true,
  "allowSyntheticDefaultImports": true,
  "strict": true,
  "noImplicitReturns": true
  },
  "include": ["./src/**/*"]
}
```

TypeScript is now set up in our project, but to truly take advantage of this within our Vue applications we should also use `vue-class-component`. This allows us to take advantage of static typing on our component properties, as well as define components as native JavaScript classes:

```
# Install TypeScript helpers
npm install vue-class-component --save-dev
```

We can then define our `App.vue` file by first specifying it as a script with the `lang="ts"` attribute. We can then import Vue as always, but as well as this, we're also importing `Component` from `vue-class-component` to be used as a decorator within this file. This allows us to specify this as a new Vue component, and using the Component decorator we can define properties, templates, and more.

Inside of our Component decorator, we're specifying a template with an input box and button. This example allows us to see how we can bind to class properties, as well as call methods from our class. The following code should replace the code already in the `App.vue` file:

```
<script lang="ts">
import Vue from 'vue';
import Component from 'vue-class-component';

@Component({
 template: `
 <div>
    <input type="text" v-model="name" />
    <button @click="sayHello(name)">Say Hello!</button>
```

```
   </div>
   `
})
export default class App extends Vue {
 name: string = 'Paul';

 sayHello(name: string): void {
   alert(`Hello ${name}`)
 }
}
</script>
```

After running the preceding code, you should get something like this:

Lifecycle hooks

Lifecycle hooks such as created(), mounted(), destroyed(), and so on can be defined as functions within the class.

- created()

    This allows for actions to be performed to a component before it is added into the DOM. Using this hook allows access to both data and events.

- `mounted()`

Mounted gives access to a component before it is rendered as well as after it has been rendered. It provides full access for interacting with the DOM and component.

- `destroyed()`

Everything that was attached to the component has been destroyed. It allows for cleanup of the component when it is removed from the DOM.

They'll be recognized and act the same way as expected without TypeScript. Here's an example when using the `created` and `mounted` hooks:

```
// Omitted
export default class App extends Vue {
 name: string = 'Paul';

 created() {
 console.log(`Created: Hello ${this.name}`)
 }

 mounted() {
 console.log(`Mounted: Hello ${this.name}`);
 }
}
```

Now if we head over to the console, we can see that the message of 'Hello' is outputted with the name of Paul:

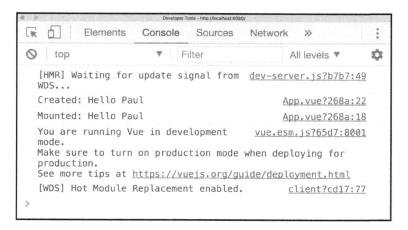

Properties

We've seen how we can create classes and use the Component decorator; let's now take a look at how we can define "props" inside of our class using the vue-property-decorator:

```
# Install Vue Property Decorator
npm install vue-property-decorator --save-dev
```

This depends on the vue-class-component, so anytime we install vue-property-decorator you'll need to ensure vue-class-component is also installed. Let's then define a Component property using the @Prop decorator:

```
<script lang="ts">
import Vue from 'vue';
import { Component, Prop } from 'vue-property-decorator';

// Omitted
@Component({
})
export default class App extends Vue {
@Prop({ default: 'Paul Halliday' }) name: string;
}
</script>
```

Notice how we're now importing the Component from 'vue-property-decorator' instead of vue-class-component. This is because it exports this as a module for us to import. We're then defining a new component property with the key of name and the default value of 'Paul Halliday'; prior to using TypeScript, it would have looked as follows:

```
export default {
 props: {
 name: {
  type: String,
  default: 'Paul Halliday'
  }
 }
}
```

Computed

Computed properties allow for multiple expressions to be passed, and these properties on the Vue instance require the use of class getters/setters. So, if we wanted to retrieve a reversed version of our name, we could simply pass the following:

```
@Component({
  template: `
    <div>
      <input type="text" v-model="name" />
      <button @click="sayHello(name)">Say Hello!</button>
      <p>{{nameReversed}}</p>
    </div>
  `
})
export default class App extends Vue {
  @Prop({ default: 'Paul Halliday' }) name: string;

  // Computed values
  get nameReversed() {
    return this.name.split("").reverse().join("");
  }

  sayHello(name: string): void {
    alert(`Hello ${name}`)
  }
}
```

This would otherwise have been equivalent to:

```
export default {
  computed: {
    nameReversed() {
      return this.name.split("").reverse().join("");
    }
  }
}
```

Other decorators can be used, such as @Watch, @Inject, @Model, and @Provide. Each decorator allows for a consistent implementation, and provides a similar API to the vanilla Vue instance. In the next section, we're going to look at how we can enhance the reactivity of our Vue applications with RxJS.

RxJS and Vue

If you come from an Angular background, you'll most likely feel right at home with *at least* the basic concepts of RxJS. This means we're usually dealing with things such as Observables, Subjects, and a variety of operators. If you haven't used them before, not to worry - we'll be investigating what RxJS is, and why we'd want to use it within Vue.

What is RxJS?

If we look at the RxJS documentation, we're greeted with the following definition: *"ReactiveX is a library for composing asynchronous and event-based programs by using observable sequences"* (http://reactivex.io/intro.html). At first glance, this is not exactly a description that makes us feel comfortable using this within our projects.

RxJS assists us in using reactive programming principles inside of our application, often referred to as a more declarative style rather than imperative. When we talk about an imperative programming style, we're usually telling the computer the exact steps of how to do a particular task. A declarative style allows us to focus more on the expected outcome rather than the implementation.

In JavaScript, we can create an `event` stream by using the following:

```
document.addEventListener('click', event => {
 console.log(event);
 });
```

This then allows us to observe any mouse clicks on the document. We can capture things such as the click coordinates, target, event type, and so on. Evidently, this is an asynchronous observable data stream. We don't know when someone is going to click the screen, nor do we care. All we do is observe and perform a particular action when that event occurs.

We can use RxJS to take these same principles and apply it to our modern day applications where everything is a stream. We could have an observable data stream of everything from a Facebook feed to document click events, timers, anything! Everything can be a stream.

Integrating with Vue

To integrate RxJS with Vue, we'll need to make a new Vue project and install both RxJS and Vue-Rx. One of the great things about using the Vue-Rx plugin is that it's officially supported by the Vue.js team, which gives us confidence that it'll be supported in the long term.

Let's create a new project with the Vue CLI, and integrate RxJS:

```
# New Vue project
vue init webpack-simple vue-rxjs

# Change directory
cd vue-rxjs

# Install dependencies
npm install

# Install rxjs and vue-rx
npm install rxjs vue-rx

# Run project
npm run dev
```

We now need to tell Vue that we'd like to use the `VueRx` plugin. This can be done using `Vue.use()`, and is not specific to this implementation. Any time we're looking to add new plugins to our Vue instance(s), calling `Vue.use()` makes an internal call to the plugin's `install()` method, extending the global scope with the new functionality. The file to edit will be our `main.js` file, which is located at `src/main.js`. We'll be looking at plugins in more detail within later chapters of this book:

```
import Vue from "vue";
import App from "./App.vue";
import VueRx from "vue-rx";
import Rx from "rxjs";

// Use the VueRx plugin with the entire RxJS library
Vue.use(VueRx, Rx);

new Vue({
 el: "#app",
 render: h => h(App)
});
```

Notice any issues with the preceding implementation? Well, in the interests of application performance and reducing bundle size, we should only import what we need. This then becomes:

```
import Vue from "vue";
import App from "./App.vue";
import VueRx from "vue-rx";

// Import only the necessary modules
import { Observable } from "rxjs/Observable";
import { Subject } from "rxjs/Subject";

// Use only Observable and Subject. Add more if needed.
Vue.use(VueRx, {
Observable,
Subject
});

new Vue({
el: "#app",
render: h => h(App)
});
```

We can then create an `Observable` data stream inside of our Vue application. Let's head over to `App.vue`, and import the necessary modules from RxJS:

```
// Required to create an Observable stream
import { Observable } from 'rxjs/Observable';
import 'rxjs/add/observable/of';
```

We can then create a new `Observable` of data; in this example, we'll be using a simple array of people:

```
// New Observable stream of string array values
const people$ = Observable.of(['Paul', 'Katie', 'Bob']);
```

This then allows us to subscribe to this `Observable` from within the subscriptions object. If you've ever used Angular before, this allows us to access the `Observable` (and handles the necessary unsubscription) similar to the Async pipe:

```
export default {
  data () {
    return {
      msg: 'Welcome to Your Vue.js App'
    }
  },
  /**
```

```
 * Bind to Observable using the subscriptions object.
 * Allows us to then access the values of people$ inside of our template.
 * Similar to the Async pipe within Angular
 **/
subscriptions: {
  people$
}
}
```

As well as this, if we wanted to create a new instance of our Observable for each component, we can instead declare our subscriptions as a function:

```
subscriptions() {
  const people$ = Observable.of(['Paul', 'Katie', 'Bob'])
  return {
    people$
  }
}
```

Finally, we can then display the results of the Observable inside of our template. We can use the v-for directive to iterate over the array and display the results on screen. How does this work? Using the following example, the v-for syntax uses an item in items syntax, which can be thought of a person in people$ in our context. This allows us to access each item inside of our people$ Observable (or any other array) with interpolation binding:

```
<template>
  <div id="app">
    <ul>
      <li
        v-for="(person,index) in people$":key="index"> {{person}}
      </li>
    </ul>
  </div>
</template>
```

As you can see inside of the browser, our three items have now appeared on the screen inside of our list item:

Iterating over RxJS Observables

Summary

In this chapter, we looked at how we can take advantage of the Vue CLI to scaffold new Vue projects with appropriate bundling configurations and ES2015 support. We've seen that not only does this give us extra power, but it also saves us a significant amount of time in the long run. We don't have to remember how to create a Webpack or Babel configuration, as this is all handled for us by the starter templates; but even still, if we want to add extra configuration options, we can.

We then looked at how we can implement TypeScript with Webpack and the `ts-loader`, as well as taking advantage of common TypeScript and Vue patterns with the property decorator(s). This allows us to take advantage of core tooling and help reduce bugs in our code.

Finally, we also implemented RxJS and Vue-Rx in our application to take advantage of the Observable pattern. If you're interested in using RxJS inside of your projects, this is a good starting point for future integrations.

In the next chapter, we're going to take a deeper look at the Vue.js instance and the different reserved properties, such as data, computed, ND watch, as well as creating getters and setters. This chapter especially considers when you should use computed to use or watch properties.

3
Writing Clean and Lean Code with Vue

In this section, we'll be investigating how a Vue.js instance works at a lower level by looking at how this is handled by Vue. We'll also be looking at the various properties on our instance such as data, computed, watch, as well as best practices when using each one. Furthermore, we'll be looking at the various lifecycle hooks available within our Vue instance, allowing us to call particular functions at various stages of our application. Finally, we'll be investigating the **Document Object Model (DOM)** and why Vue implements a Virtual DOM for enhanced performance.

By the end of this chapter you will:

- Have a greater understanding of how `this` keyword works within JavaScript
- Understand how Vue proxies `this` keyword within Vue instances
- Use data properties to create reactive bindings
- Use computed properties to create declarative functions based on our data model
- Use watched properties to access asynchronous data and build upon the foundations of computed properties
- Use lifecycle hooks to activate functionality at particular stages of the Vue lifecycle
- Investigate the DOM and Virtual DOM for an understanding of how Vue renders data to the screen

To begin, let's start off by looking into how this works within JavaScript and how this relates to the context within our Vue instances.

Proxying

So far, you may have interacted with a Vue application and thought to yourself: How does `this` work the way it does? Before looking into how Vue.js handles `this`, let's have a look at how it works within JavaScript.

How 'this' works within JavaScript

Within JavaScript, `this` has varying contexts that range from the global window context to eval, newable, and function contexts. As the default context for this relates to the global scope, this is our window object:

```
/**
 * Outputting the value of this to the console in the global context
returns the Window object
 */
console.log(this);

/**
 * When referencing global Window objects, we don't need to refer to them
with this, but if we do, we get the same behavior
 */
alert('Alert one');
this.alert('Alert two');
```

The context of this changes depending on where we are in scope. This means, that if we had a `Student` object with particular values, such as `firstName`, `lastName`, `grades`, and so on, the context of `this` would be related to the object itself:

```
/**
 * The context of this changes when we enter another lexical scope, take
our Student object example:
 */
const Student = {
 firstName: 'Paul',
 lastName: 'Halliday',
 grades: [50, 95, 70, 65, 35],
 getFullName() {
  return `${this.firstName} ${this.lastName}`
```

```
  },
  getGrades() {
    return this.grades.reduce((accumulator, grade) => accumulator + grade);
  },
  toString() {
    return `Student ${this.getFullName()} scored ${this.getGrades()}/500`;
  }
}
```

When we run the preceding code with `console.log(Student.toString())`, we get this:
`Student Paul Halliday scored 315/500` as the context of this is now scoped to the object itself rather than the global window scope.

If we wanted to display this in the document we could do it like so:

```
let res = document.createTextNode(Student.toString());
let heading = document.createElement('h1');
heading.appendChild(res);
document.body.appendChild(heading);
```

Notice that, with the preceding code, once again we don't have to use `this` as it isn't needed with the global context.

Now that we have an understanding of how `this` works at a basic level, we can investigate how Vue proxies `this` inside of our instances to make interacting with the various properties much easier.

How Vue handles 'this'

You may have noticed up to this point that we're able to reference values inside of our data, methods, and other objects using `this` syntax, but the actual structure of our instance is `this.data.propertyName` or `this.methods.methodName`; all of this is possible due to the way Vue proxies our instance properties.

Let's take a very simple Vue application that has one instance. We have a `data` object that has a `message` variable and a method named `showAlert`; how does Vue know how to access our alert text with `this.message`?

```
<template>
 <button @click="showAlert">
 Show Alert</button>
</template>

<script>
```

```
export default {
 data() {
  return {
   message: 'Hello World!',
  };
 },
 methods: {
  showAlert() {
   alert(this.message);
  },
 },
};
</script>
```

Vue proxies the instance properties to the top level object, allowing us to access these properties via this. If we were to log out the instance to the console (with the help of Vue.js devtools), we'd get the following result:

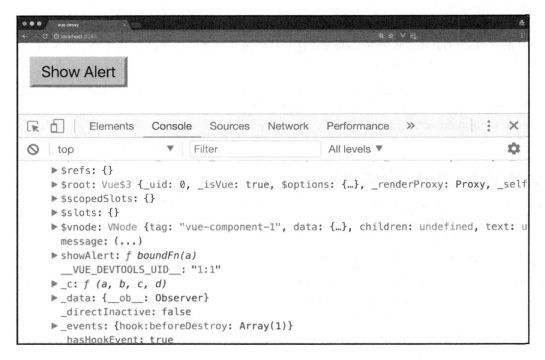

Console logout

The key properties to look at within the preceding screenshot are `message` and `showAlert`, both of which are defined on our Vue instance yet proxied to the root object instance at initialization time.

Data properties

When we add a variable to our data object, we're essentially creating a reactive property that updates the view any time it changes. This means that, if we had a data object with a property named `firstName`, that property would be re-rendered on the screen each time the value changes:

```
<!DOCTYPE html>
<html>
<head>
 <title>Vue Data</title>
 <script src="https://unpkg.com/vue"></script>
</head>
<body>
 <div id="app">
  <h1>Name: {{ firstName }}</h1>
  <input type="text" v-model="firstName">
 </div>

 <script>
 const app = new Vue({
  el: '#app',
  data: {
   firstName: 'Paul'
  }
 });
 </script>
</body>
</html>
```

This reactivity does not extend to objects added to our Vue instance after the instance has been created outside of the data object. If we had another example of this, but this time including appending another property such as `fullName` to the instance itself:

```
<body>
 <div id="app">
  <h1>Name: {{ firstName }}</h1>
  <h1>Name: {{ name }}</h1>
  <input type="text" v-model="firstName">
 </div>
```

```
<script>
const app = new Vue({
 el: '#app',
 data: {
  firstName: 'Paul'
 }
});
app.fullName = 'Paul Halliday';
</script>
</body>
```

Even though this item is on the root instance (the same as our firstName variable), fullName is not reactive and will not re-render upon any changes. This does not work because, when the Vue instance is initialized, it maps over each one of the properties and adds a getter and setter to each data property, thus, if we add a new property after initialization, it lacks this and is not reactive.

How does Vue achieve reactive properties? Currently, it uses Object.defineProperty to define a custom getter/setter for items inside of the instance. Let's create our own property on an object with standard get/set features:

```
const user = {};
let fullName = 'Paul Halliday';

Object.defineProperty(user, 'fullName', {
 configurable: true,
 enumerable: true,
 get() {
  return fullName;
 },
 set(v) {
  fullName = v;
 }
});

console.log(user.fullName); // > Paul Halliday
user.fullName = "John Doe";
console.log(user.fullName); // > John Doe
```

As the watchers are set with a custom property setter/getter, merely adding a property to the instance after initialization doesn't allow for reactivity. This is likely to change within Vue 3 as it will be using the newer ES2015+ Proxy API (but potentially lacking support for older browsers).

There's more to our Vue instance than a data property! Let's use computed to create reactive, derived values based on items inside of our data model.

Computed properties

In this section, we'll be looking at computed properties within our Vue instance. This allows us to create small, declarative functions that return a singular value based on items inside of our data model. Why is this important? Well, if we kept all of our logic inside of our templates, both our team members and our future self would have to do more work to understand what our application does.

Therefore, we can use computed properties to vastly simplify our templates and create variables that we can reference instead of the logic itself. It goes further than an abstraction; computed properties are cached and will not be recalculated unless a dependency has changed.

Let's create a simple project to see this in action:

```
# Create a new Vue.js project
$ vue init webpack-simple computed

# Change directory
$ cd computed

# Install dependencies
$ npm install

# Run application
$ npm run dev
```

Interpolation is powerful; for example, inside of our Vue.js templates we can take a string (for example, firstName) and reverse this using the reverse() method:

```
<h1>{{ firstName.split('').reverse().join('') }}</h1>
```

We'll now be showing a reversed version of our firstName, so **Paul** would become **luaP**. The issue with this is that it's not very practical to keep logic inside of our templates. If we'd like to reverse multiple fields, we have to then add another split(), reverse(), and join() on each property. To make this more declarative, we can use computed properties.

Inside of App.vue, we can add a new computed object, that contains a function named reversedName; this takes our logic for reversing our string and allows us to abstract this into a function containing logic that would otherwise pollute the template:

```
<template>
 <h1>Name: {{ reversedName }}</h1>
</template>

<script>
export default {
 data() {
   return {
     firstName: 'Paul'
   }
 },
 computed: {
   reversedName() {
     return this.firstName.split('').reverse().join('')
   }
 }
}
</script>
```

We could then see more information about our computed properties within Vue.js devtools:

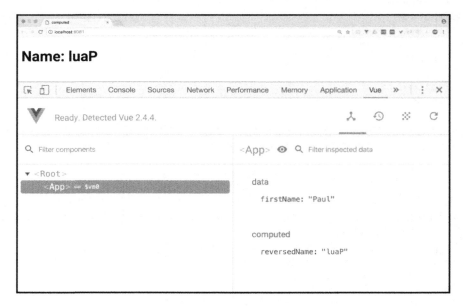

Using devtools to display data

In our simple example, it's important to realize that, while we could make this a method, there are reasons why we should keep this as a computed property. Computed properties are cached and are not re-rendered unless their dependency changes, which is especially important if we have a larger data-driven application.

Watched properties

Computed properties are not always the answer to our reactive data problems, sometimes we need to create our own custom watched properties. Computed properties can only be synchronous, must be pure (for example, no observed side-effects), and return a value; this is in direct contrast to a watched property, which is often used to deal with asynchronous data.

A watched property allows us to reactively execute a function whenever a piece of data changes. This means that we can call a function every time an item from our data object changes, and we'll have access to this changed value as a parameter. Let's take a look at this with a simple example:

 Note: Axios is a library that will need to be added to the project. To do so, head to https://github.com/axios/axios and follow the installation steps provided.

```
<template>
 <div>
  <input type="number" v-model="id" />
  <p>Name: {{user.name}}</p>
  <p>Email: {{user.email}}</p>
  <p>Id: {{user.id}}</p>
 </div>
</template>

<script>
import axios from 'axios';

export default {
 data() {
  return {
   id: '',
   user: {}
  }
 },
 methods: {
```

```
getDataForUser() {
  axios.get(`https://jsonplaceholder.typicode.com/users/${this.id}`)
.then(res => this.user = res.data);
  }
},
watch: {
  id() {
    this.getDataForUser();
  }
 }
}
</script>
```

In this example, any time our text box changes with a new id (1-10), we get information about that particular user, like so:

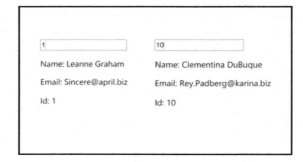

This is effectively watching for any changes on the id and calling the getDataForUser method, retrieving new data about this user.

Although watched properties do have a lot of power, the benefits of computed properties on performance and ease of use should not be understated; therefore wherever possible, favor computed properties over watched properties.

Lifecycle hooks

We have access to a variety of lifecycle hooks that fire at particular points during the creation of our Vue instance. These hooks range from prior to creation with beforeCreate, to after the instance is mounted, destroyed, and many more in between.

As the following figure shows, the creation of a new Vue instance fires off functions at varying stages of the instance lifecycle.

We'll be looking at how we can activate these hooks within this section:

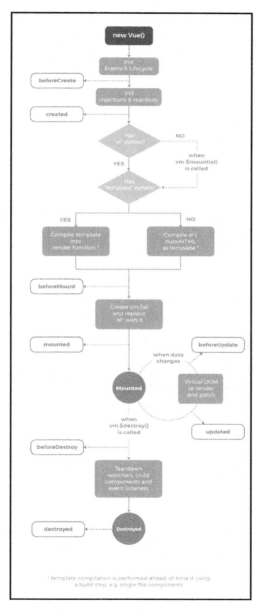

Vue.js instance lifecycle hooks

Taking advantage of the lifecycle hooks (https://vuejs.org/v2/guide/instance.html) can be done in a similar way to any other property on our Vue instance. Let's take a look at how we can interact with each one of the hooks, starting from the top; I'll be creating another project based on the standard webpack-simple template:

```
// App.vue
<template>
</template>

<script>
export default {
 data () {
   return {
    msg: 'Welcome to Your Vue.js App'
   }
 },
 beforeCreate() {
  console.log('beforeCreate');
 },
 created() {
  console.log('created');
 }
}
</script>
```

Notice how we've simply added these functions to our instance without any extra imports or syntax. We then get two different log statements in our console, one prior to the creation of our instance and one after it has been created. The next stage for our instance is the beforeMounted and mounted hooks; if we add these, we'll be able to see a message on the console once again:

```
beforeMount() {
 console.log('beforeMount');
},
mounted() {
 console.log('mounted');
}
```

If we then modified our template so it had a button that updated one of our data properties, we'd be able to fire a beforeUpdated and updated hook:

```
<template>
 <div>
  <h1>{{msg}}</h1>
  <button @click="msg = 'Updated Hook'">Update Message</button>
 </div>
```

```
</template>

<script>
export default {
 data () {
   return {
    msg: 'Welcome to Your Vue.js App'
   }
 },
 beforeCreate() {
  console.log('beforeCreate');
 },
 created() {
  console.log('created');
 },
 beforeMount() {
  console.log('beforeMount');
 },
 mounted() {
  console.log('mounted');
 },
 beforeUpdated() {
  console.log('beforeUpdated');
 },
 updated() {
  console.log('updated');
 }
}
</script>
```

Whenever we select the `Update Message` button, our `beforeUpdated` and `updated` hooks both fire. This allows us to perform an action at this stage in the lifecycle, leaving us only with `beforeDestroy` and destroyed yet to cover. Let's add a button and a method to our instance that call `$destroy`, allowing us to trigger the appropriate lifecycle hook:

```
<template>
  <div>
    <h1>{{msg}}</h1>
    <button @click="msg = 'Updated Hook'">Update Message
    </button>
    <button @click="remove">Destroy instance</button>
  </div>
</template>
```

We can then add the `remove` method to our instance, as well as the functions that allow us to capture the appropriate hooks:

```
methods: {
  remove(){
    this.$destroy();
  }
},
// Other hooks
  beforeDestroy(){
  console.log("Before destroy");
},
  destroyed(){
  console.log("Destroyed");
}
```

When we select the `destroy` instance button, the `beforeDestroy` and `destroy` lifecycle hooks will fire. This allows us to clean up any subscriptions or perform any other action(s) when destroying an instance. In a real-world scenario, lifecycle control should be left up to data-driven directives, such as `v-if` and `v-for`. We'll be looking at these directives in more detail in the next chapter.

Vue.js and the Virtual DOM

On the topic of performance improvements, let's consider why Vue.js makes extensive use of the Virtual DOM to render our elements on the screen. Before looking at the Virtual DOM, we need to have a foundational understanding of what the DOM actually is.

DOM

The DOM is what is used to describe the structure of an HTML or XML page. It creates a tree-like structure that provides us with the ability to do everything from creating, reading, updating, and deleting nodes to traversing the tree and many more features, all within JavaScript. Let's consider the following HTML page:

```
<!DOCTYPE html>
<html lang="en">
<head>
 <title>DOM Example</title>
</head>
<body>
 <div>
```

```
    <p>I love JavaScript!</p>
    <p>Here's a list of my favourite frameworks:</p>
    <ul>
      <li>Vue.js</li>
      <li>Angular</li>
      <li>React</li>
    </ul>
  </div>

  <script src="app.js"></script>
</body>
</html>
```

We're able to look at the HTML and see that we have one **div**, two **p**, one **ul**, and **li** tags. The browser parses this HTML and produces the DOM Tree, which at a high level looks similar to this:

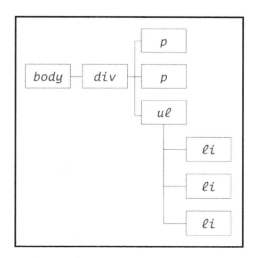

We can then interact with the DOM to get access to these elements by `TagName` using `document.getElementsByTagName()`, returning a HTML collection. If we wanted to map over these collection objects, we could create an array of these elements using `Array.from`. The following is an example:

```
const paragraphs = Array.from(document.getElementsByTagName('p'));
const listItems = Array.from(document.getElementsByTagName('li'));

paragraphs.map(p => console.log(p.innerHTML));
listItems.map(li => console.log(li.innerHTML));
```

This should then log the `innerHTML` of each item to the console inside of our array(s), thus showing how we can access items inside of the DOM:

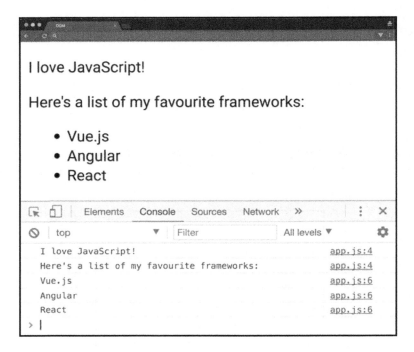

Virtual DOM

Updating DOM nodes is computationally expensive and depending on the size of your application, this can substantially slow down the performance of your application. The Virtual DOM takes the concept of the DOM and provides us an abstraction, which allows for a diffing algorithm to be used to update DOM nodes. To fully take advantage of this, these nodes are no longer accessed with the document prefix and instead are often represented as JavaScript objects.

This allows Vue to work out exactly *what* changed and only re-render items in the actual DOM that is different from the previous.

Summary

In this chapter, we learned more about the Vue instance and how we can take advantage of a variety of property types such as data, watchers, computed values, and more. We've learned about how `this` works in JavaScript and the differences when using it inside of a Vue instance. Furthermore, we've investigated the DOM and why Vue uses the Virtual DOM to create performant applications.

In summary, data properties allow for reactive properties within our templates, computed properties allow us to take our template and filtering logic and separate it into performant properties that can be accessed within our templates, and watched properties allow us to work with the complexities of asynchronous operations.

In the next chapter, we'll be taking an in-depth look at Vue directives, such as `v-if`, `v-model`, `v-for`, and how they can be used to create powerful reactive applications.

4
Vue.js Directives

When writing Vue applications, we have access to a variety of powerful directives that allow us to shape the way our content appears on the screen. This allows us to craft highly interactive user experiences with additions to our HTML templates. This chapter will be looking at each one of these directives in detail, as well as any shortcuts and patterns that allow us to improve our workflow.

By the end of this chapter you will have:

- Used attribute binding to conditionally change element behavior
- Investigated two-way binding with `v-model`
- Conditionally displayed information with `v-if`, `v-else`, and `v-if-else`
- Iterated over items in a collection with `v-for`
- Listened to events (such as keyboard/input) with `v-on`
- Used event modifiers to change the binding of a directive
- Used filters to change the view data of a binding
- Looked at how we can use shorthand syntax to save time and be more declarative

Model

One of the most common requirements for any business application is text input. Vue assists us with this need with the `v-model` directive. It allows us to create reactive two-way data bindings on form input events, making working with forms easily. It's a welcome abstraction over what would otherwise be a tedious way to get form values and input events. To explore this, we can create a new Vue project:

```
# Create a new Vue project
```

```
$ vue init webpack-simple vue-model

# Navigate to directory
$ cd vue-model

# Install dependencies
$ npm install

# Run application
$ npm run dev
```

We can head over to our root `App.vue` file and remove everything from the template and instead add a new `div` that encompasses a `label` and `form` input:

```
<template>
 <div id="app">
  <label>Name:</label>
  <input type="text">
 </div>
</template>
```

This gives us the ability to add text to our input element, that is, prompting the user to input their name. I'd like to capture this value and display it below the name element for demonstration sake. In order to do this, we'd need to add the `v-model` directive to the input element; this will allow us to capture the user input events and place the value into a variable. We'll call this variable `name` and subsequently add it to our `data` object within our Vue instance. As the value is now captured as a variable, we can display this in our template with interpolation binding:

```
<template>
  <div id="app">
    <label>Name:</label>
    <input type="text" v-model="name">
    <p>{{name}}</p>
  </div>
</template>

<script>
export default {
  data () {
    return {
     name: ''
    }
  }
}
</script>
```

The result can be seen in the following screenshot:

We're not limited to working with text inputs when using v-model, we can also capture radio buttons or checkboxes when selected. The following example shows this:

```
<input type="checkbox" v-model="checked">
<span>Am I checked? {{checked ? 'Yes' : 'No' }}</span>
```

This will then display in our browser like so:

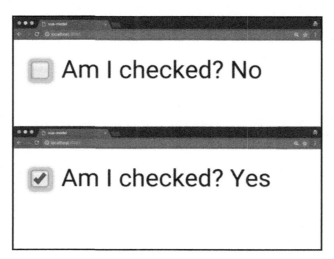

The great thing about `v-model` is that it's highly adaptable to a variety of form controls, giving us declarative power over our HTML templates.

Iteration with v-for

If we have content that we'd like to repeat over a certain number, we can use `v-for`. This is often used to populate a template with a dataset. For example, let's say we have a list of groceries and we wanted to display this list on the screen; we could do this with `v-for`. We can create a new project to see this in action:

```
# Create a new Vue project
$ vue init webpack-simple vue-for

# Navigate to directory
$ cd vue-for

# Install dependencies
$ npm install

# Run application
$ npm run dev
```

To start with, let's create an array with a list of groceries that we can display on screen. Each item has an `id`, `name`, and `quantity`:

```
<script>
export default {
  name: 'app',
  data () {
    return {
      groceries: [
        {
          id: 1,
          name: 'Pizza',
          quantity: 1
        },
        {
          id: 2,
          name: 'Hot Sauce',
          quantity: 5
        },
        {
          id: 3,
          name: 'Salad',
```

```
              quantity: 1
          },
          {
              id: 4,
              name: 'Water',
              quantity: 1
          },
          {
              id: 4,
              name: 'Yoghurt',
              quantity: 1
          }
      ]
    }
  }
}
</script>

<style>
#app {
  font-family: 'Avenir', Helvetica, Arial, sans-serif;
  -webkit-font-smoothing: antialiased;
  -moz-osx-font-smoothing: grayscale;
  text-align: center;
  color: #2c3e50;
  margin-top: 60px;
}

ul {
  list-style-type: none;
  padding: 0;
}

li {
  display: block;
}

</style>
```

We can then iterate over each item inside of our groceries list and modify the DOM to display them on screen:

```
<template>
  <div id="app">
    <h1>Shopping List</h1>
    <ul>
      <li v-for="item in groceries" v-bind:key="item.id">
        {{item.name}}
```

```
        </li>
      </ul>
    </div>
  </template>
```

Notice how we have a v-bind:key="item.id" on the li element. This makes Vue work better with iterations that change over time and a key should be added where possible:

Bindings

In this section, we're going to look at how we can dynamically toggle CSS classes within our Vue applications. We'll start off by investigating the v-bind directive and we'll see how this can be applied to both class and style attributes. This is great for conditionally applying styles based on a particular business logic. Let's create a new Vue project for this example:

```
# Create a new Vue project
$ vue init webpack-simple vue-bind

# Navigate to directory
$ cd vue-bind

# Install dependencies
$ npm install

# Run application
$ npm run dev
```

Inside of our project, we can make checkboxes that represent the different states of our application. We'll start off with one named `red`. As you may be able to infer, by checking this we can turn a particular piece of text `red` in color and subsequently turn it black by unchecking it.

Create a `data` object named `red` with the value of `false` inside `App.vue`:

```
<script>
export default {
 data () {
  return {
   red: false
  }
 }
}
</script>
```

This represent the value of our checkbox, which we'll be able to set with the `v-model` directive:

```
<template>
 <div id="app">
  <h1>Vue Bindings</h1>

  <input type="checkbox" v-model="red" >
  <span>Red</span>
 </div>
</template>
```

At this point, we can create a new CSS class for our color:

```
<style>
.red {
 color: red;
}
</style>
```

As you can see in the browser if we open the dev tools, we can see that the color of the text is currently set to `blue`:

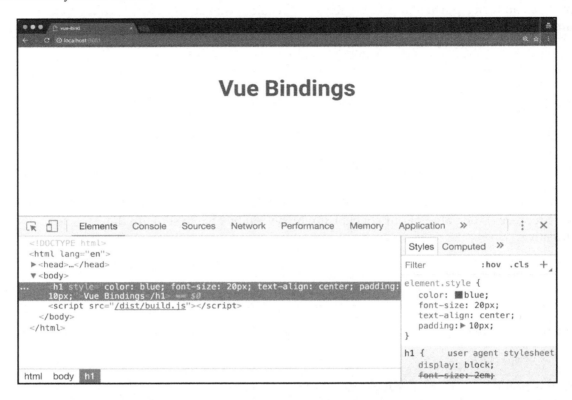

Finally, to add the addition/removal of the class based on the context of the `red` variable, we'll need to add the `v-bind:class` directive to our `h1` like so:

```
<h1 v-bind:class="{ 'red': red }">Vue Bindings</h1>
```

Now in our browser, we can see that we have the ability to check the box to set the text to
`red` like so:

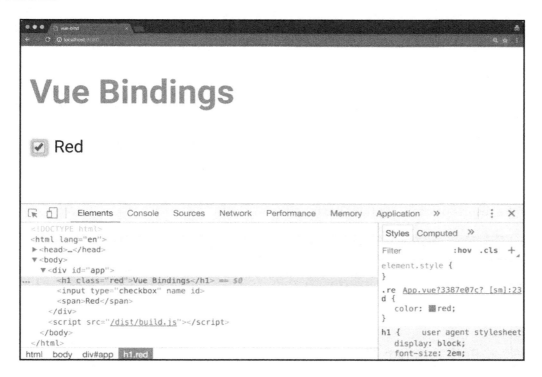

Adding secondary properties

If we also wanted to add another property to our class binding, we'd need to add another
property (such as `strikeThrough`) to our `data` object like so:

```
data () {
 return {
  red: false,
  strikeThrough: false
 }
}
```

We can then add another `checkbox`:

```
<input type="checkbox" v-model="strikeThrough">
<span>Strike Through</span>
```

With an appropriate `style`:

```
<style>
.red {
 color: red;
}

.strike-through {
 text-decoration: line-through;
}
</style>
```

Finally, we then need to adjust our binding to add the extra class like so:

```
<h1 v-bind:class="{ 'red': red, 'strike-through': strikeThrough }">Vue
Bindings</h1>
```

Here's the results of checking both boxes:

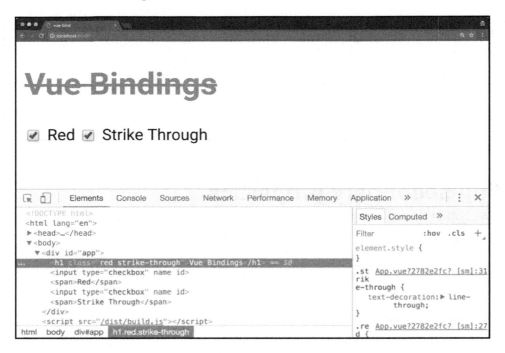

Style bindings

We may want to add various styles to our heading, so instead, we could use `v-bind:style`. We can see this in action by creating a new object named `headingStyles` inside of our `data` object:

```
data () {
 return {
  headingStyles: {
   color: 'blue',
   fontSize: '20px',
   textAlign: 'center'
  }
 }
}
```

Anytime we're adding CSS classes that would otherwise be kebab-case (for example, `text-align`) they now become camel-case (`textAlign`) inside of our JavaScript.

Let's add the style to our heading inside of the template:

```
<h1 v-bind:style="headingStyles">Vue Bindings</h1>
```

Every time the compiler sees a `v-bind` or `:` the content inside of " is treated as JavaScript with an implicit `this`.

We could also split this to add `layoutStyles` as a separate object, for example:

```
data () {
 return {
  headingStyles: {
   color: 'blue',
   fontSize: '20px',
  },
  layoutStyles: {
   textAlign: 'center',
   padding: '10px'
  }
 }
}
```

So all that we have to do at this point is add the `styles` in an array within the `template` like so within the `<h1>` tag, using `v-bind`:

```
<template>
 <h1 v-bind:style="[headingStyles, layoutStyles]">Vue Bindings</h1>
</template>
```

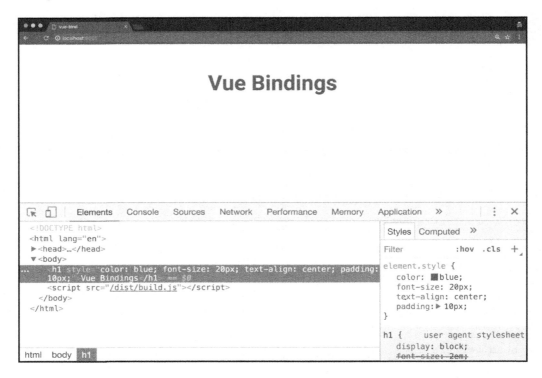

You can now see the results of our styling on screen. Note that any items further in the array will take styling preference over items declared first.

DOM events and v-on

We can handle DOM events within Vue by using v-on. By listening to DOM events, we're able to react to user input with everything from key-down events (such as clicking the *Enter* button) to button click events and more.

Let's make a playground project to try this in our own project:

```
# Create a new Vue project
$ vue init webpack-simple vue-on

# Navigate to directory
$ cd vue-on

# Install dependencies
$ npm install

# Run application
$ npm run dev
```

Let's imagine an input box such that, when we either hit the **Add** button or hit the *Enter* key, the input gets added to an array:

```
<template>
 <div id="app">
  <ul>
   <li v-for="(p, index) in person" :key="index">
    {{p}}
   </li>
  </ul>
  <input type="text" v-model="person" v-on:keyup.enter="addPerson" />
  <button v-on:click="addPerson">Add {{ person}} </button>
 </div>
</template>

<script>
export default {
 name: 'app',
 data () {
  return {
   person: '',
   people: []
  }
 },
 methods: {
  addPerson() {
   this.people = this.people.concat(
```

```
      {id: this.people.length, name: this.person}
    );
  this.person = '';
  }
 }
}
</script>
```

You will have to copy the object before pushing it in.

What exactly is happening here? We're capturing the value of the user input inside of the person string using the v-model directive; after that we're listening for both keyup.enter and v-on:click events, both of which call the addPerson function, and subsequently adding the person to an array. After that, using the v-for directive, we're able to output this list of people to the page:

Key modifiers

We're not limited to simply using the enter modifier, we also have access to a variety of shorthand modifiers, for example the use of the @ symbol and shortening v-on:event.name v-on: by replacing it with the @ symbol. Other shortening methods include:

- @ is the same as v-on:

- @keyup.13 is the same as @keyup.enter
- @key* can be queued, such as @keyup.ctrl.alt.delete

Other modifiers can be seen in the following table:

Name	Description	Code Example
.enter	Whenever the *Enter* key is tapped.	`<input v-on:keyup.enter="myFunction" />`
.tab	Whenever the *Tab* key is tapped.	`<input v-on:keyup.tab="myFunction" />`
.delete	Whenever the *Delete* or *Backspace* key is tapped.	`<input v-on:keyup.delete="myFunction" />`
.esc	Whenever the *Esc* key is tapped.	`<input v-on:keyup.esc="myFunction" />`
.up	Whenever the up arrow key is tapped.	`<input v-on:keyup.up="myFunction" />`
.down	Whenever the down arrow key is tapped.	`<input v-on:keyup.down="myFunction" />`
.left	Whenever the left arrow key is tapped.	`<input v-on:keyup.left="myFunction" />`
.right	Whenever the right arrow key is tapped.	`<input v-on:keyup.right="myFunction" />`

Event modifiers

Often when we're working with events inside of JavaScript, we'll modify the functionality of the event itself. This means that we need to add `event.preventDefault()` or `event.stopPropagation()` within our handler. Vue helps us abstract these calls by handling this inside of the template using event modifiers.

This is best shown with a `form` example. Let's take our previous people example and modify this to contain a `form` element:

```
<template>
  <div id="app">
    <ul>
      <li v-for="p in people" v-bind:key="p.id" >
        {{p}}
      </li>
    </ul>

    <form v-on:submit="addPerson">
      <input type="text" v-model="person" />
      <button>Add {{ person}} </button>
    </form>
  </div>
</template>
```

If you try and run this example, you'll notice that when we click the **Add** button, the page refreshes. This is because it's the default behavior of the `form` submitted event. As we're not POSTing data to a server at this point, we instead need to add the `.prevent` modifier to our `submit` event:

```
<form v-on:submit.prevent="addPerson">
  <input type="text" v-model="person" />
  <button>Add {{ person}} </button>
</form>
```

Now when we select our button, the `addPerson` function is called without refreshing the page.

Conditionally showing DOM elements

When creating business applications, there'll be many times when you only want to display a particular element if a certain condition is **true** or **false**. This could include a user's age, whether the user is logged in, whether it is an administrator or any other piece of business logic you can think of.

For this, we have a variety of conditional directives such as v-show, v-if, v-else, and v-else-if, all of which act in similar yet different ways. Let's take a look at this in more detail by creating a new playground project:

```
# Create a new Vue project
$ vue init webpack-simple vue-conditionals

# Navigate to directory
$ cd vue-conditionals

# Install dependencies
$ npm install

# Run application
$ npm run dev
```

v-show

If we want to hide elements from view yet still have them in the DOM (effectively display:none), we can use v-show:

```
<template>
<div id="app">
 <article v-show="admin">
  <header>Protected Content</header>
 <section class="main">
  <h1>If you can see this, you're an admin!</h1>
 </section>
</article>

 <button @click="admin = !admin">Flip permissions</button>
</div>
</template>

<script>
export default{
name: 'app',
 data (){
  return{
   admin: true
     }
   }
}
</script>
```

For example, if we had a data variable that allowed us to determine whether someone was an administrator, we'd be able to use `v-show` to only show protected content to appropriate users:

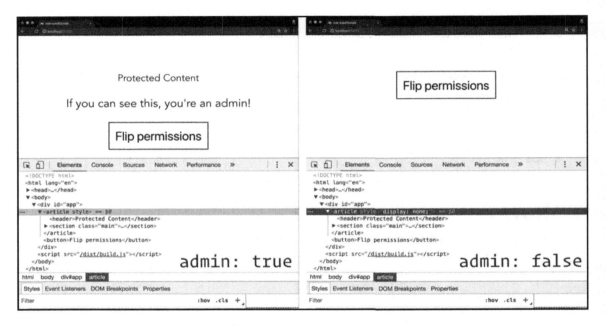

Notice how, in the preceding figure when `admin` is set to `false`, the `display: none` style is added to the element. At first glance it may seem like this is exactly what we want, our item has disappeared! In certain circumstances, this is the case, but in other scenarios, the use of `v-if` may be better.

`v-show` doesn't remove the element from the DOM, meaning that everything is initially loaded and simply hidden if it isn't being used. Our page will have to render this content and this could cause performance issues when used in the wrong way; therefore prior to using `v-show` ask this question:

> *Do I need to show this component again? If so, will be showing it often?*

If the answer to this question is **yes**, then `v-show` may be better in this circumstance. Otherwise, if the answer to this is **no**, then `v-if` may be better in this use case.

v-if

If we'd like to conditionally remove the element from the DOM, we can use `v-if`. Let's replace our previous `v-show` directive with `v-if`:

```
<article v-if="admin">
 <header>Protected Content</header>
 <section class="main">
  <h1>If you can see this, you're an admin!</h1>
 </section>
</article>
```

Notice that now when we look at the DOM, the element is entirely removed:

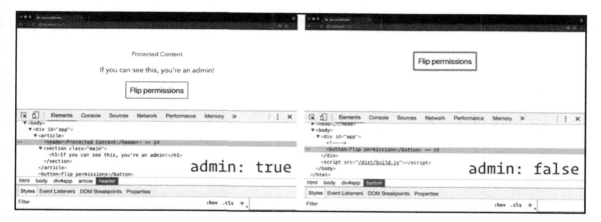

v-else

A common pattern when showing or hiding elements is to instead show a different piece of content. Whilst we could use `v-if` or `v-show` multiple times, we also have access to the `v-else` directive, which can be used directly after showing or hiding the element.

Let's take a look at this in more detail:

```
<article v-if="admin">
  <header>Protected Content</header>
  <section class="main">
    <h1>If you can see this, you're an admin!</h1>
  </section>
</article>
<article v-else>
```

```
<header>You're not an admin!</header>
<section class="main">
  <h1>Perhaps you shouldn't be here.</h1>
</section>
</article>
```

By adding the `v-else` directive to the second `<article>`, we're telling Vue that we want to show this DOM element whenever the first condition is hidden. Because of the way this works, we don't have to pass a value to `v-else` as Vue is specifically looking for a structural directive in the preceding element.

It's important to realize that this wouldn't work if we had an element in between the `v-if` and `v-else` directive(s), such as this:

```
<article v-if="admin">
  <header>Protected Content</header>
  <section class="main">
    <h1>If you can see this, you're an admin!</h1>
  </section>
</article>
<h1>The v-else will be ignored.</h1>
<article v-else>
  <header>You're not an admin!</header>
  <section class="main">
    <h1>Perhaps you shouldn't be here.</h1>
  </section>
</article>
```

v-else-if

Whilst `v-else` works well in standard **IF NOT A** then **B** scenarios, you may want to test for multiple values and show a different template. Similar to `v-else`, we can use `v-else-if` to change the behavior of our application. For this example, we'll have fun by using a generator as introduced with ES2015.

To use the generator, we'll need to install the `babel-polyfill` package; this also allows us to use things such as `async` and `await` better promise handling:

```
$ npm install babel-polyfill --save-dev
```

After installing it, we can modify our Webpack configuration (`webpack.config.js`) to include it inside of our entry files:

```
module.exports = {
 entry: ['babel-polyfill', './src/main.js'],
 output: {
  path: path.resolve(__dirname, './dist'),
  publicPath: '/dist/',
  filename: 'build.js',
 },
 // Omitted
```

If we hadn't installed the appropriate polyfill, we'd not be able to use the generator functionality within our project. Let's make a new method named `returnRole()` that gives us one of three users "roles" when called:

```
export default {
 name: 'app',
 data() {
  return {
   role: '',
  }
 },
  methods: {
    *returnRole() {
     yield 'guest';
     yield 'user';
     yield 'admin';
   }
  }
};
```

If you've never seen a generator function before, you may be wondering what the asterisk (*) is that we've prefixed to our function name, as well as the `yield` keyword. This essentially allows us to step through the function by capturing an instance of it. For example, let's make a data value that returns our iterator, which we can call `next()` on:

```
data() {
 return {
  role: '',
  roleList: this.returnRole()
 }
},
methods: {
 getRole() {
  /**
   * Calling this.roleList.next() gives us an Iterator object with the
```

```
interface of:
    * { value: string, done: boolean}
    * We can therefore check to see whether this was the >last< yielded
value with done, or get the result by calling .value
    */

    this.role = this.roleList.next().value;
},
```

We can, therefore, make a template that takes advantage of `v-if-else` by displaying different messages depending on the user role:

```
<template>
 <div id="app">
  <article v-if="role === 'admin'">
   <header>You're an admin!</header>
   <section class="main">
    <h1>If you can see this, you're an admin!</h1>
   </section>
  </article>
  <article v-else-if="role === 'user'">
   <header>You're a user!</header>
   <section class="main">
    <h1>Enjoy your stay!</h1>
   </section>
  </article>
 <article v-else-if="role === 'guest'">
  <header>You're a guest!</header>
  <section class="main">
   <h1>Maybe you should make an account.</h1>
  </section>
 </article>
 <h1 v-else>You have no role!</h1>
 <button @click="getRole()">Switch Role</button>
 </div>
</template>
```

There are different messages shown on the screen depending on the user role. If the user has no role, we use `v-else` to show a message stating `You have no role!`. This example shows how we can take advantage of structural directives to truly change the DOM depending on our application state.

Filters

In this section, we're going to investigate filters; you may have come across filters before in frameworks such as Angular (Pipes). Perhaps we want to create a filter that allows us to format a date in a readable format (DD/MM/YYYY). Let's create a playground project to investigate this further:

```
# Create a new Vue project
$ vue init webpack-simple vue-filters

# Navigate to directory
$ cd vue-filters

# Install dependencies
$ npm install

# Run application
$ npm run dev
```

If we had some test people and used the v-for directive to display them on screen, we'd get the following result:

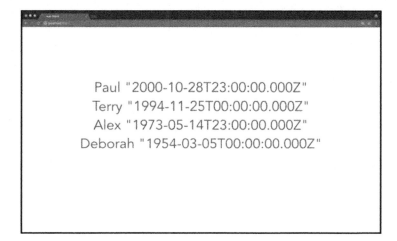

To obtain the result shown in the preceding screenshot, where we display our test people with the appropriate data through the `v-for` directive, we would have to add the following code:

```
<template>
 <div id="app">
  <ul>
   <li v-for="person in people" v-bind:key="person.id">
    {{person.name}} {{person.dob}}
   </li>
  </ul>
 </div>
</template>

<script>
export default {
 name: 'app',
 data() {
  return {
   people: [
    {
     id: 1,
     name: 'Paul',
     dob: new Date(2000, 5, 29),
    },
    {
     id: 2,
     name: 'Terry',
     dob: new Date(1994, 10, 25),
    },
    {
     id: 3,
     name: 'Alex',
     dob: new Date(1973, 4, 15),
    },
    {
     id: 4,
     name: 'Deborah',
     dob: new Date(1954, 2, 5),
    },
   ],
  };
 },
};
</script>
```

We could do the work of converting the date ourselves, but where possible it's always worth looking to see if there is a trusted third-party component that can do the same thing. We'll be using moment (https://momentjs.com) to do this.

Let's install moment for our project:

```
$ npm install moment --save
```

We can then add it to our App.vue:

```
<script>
import moment from 'moment';

export default {
 // Omitted
}
</script>
```

Locally registered filters

We then have a choice: add the filter locally to this Vue instance, or add it globally to the entire project. We'll first look at how to add it locally:

First, we'll create a function that takes in a value and returns the date as a formatted date using moment:

```
const convertDateToString = value =>
moment(String(value)).format('MM/DD/YYYY');
```

We can then add a filters object to our Vue instance and reference this by a key, such as date. When we call the date filter inside of our template, the value will be passed to this filter and instead, we'll display the converted date on screen. This can be done by using the | key, as seen in the following code:

```
<ul>
 <li v-for="person in people" v-bind:key="person.id">
  {{person.name}} {{person.dob | date}}
 </li>
</ul>
```

Finally, to add this to the local Vue instance, we can add a `filters` object that references our function:

```
export default {
 filters: {
  date: convertDateToString,
 },
```

The result of this shows the date as intended:

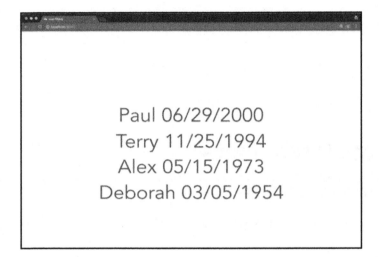

Globally registered filters

If we wanted to use this filter elsewhere, we could abstract this function into its own file and reference our filter once again, or, we could register the `date` filter globally inside of our application. Let's abstract our `convertDateToString` function into its own file at `src/filters/date/date.filter.js`:

```
import moment from 'moment';

export const convertDateToString = value =>
 moment(String(value)).format('MM/DD/YYYY');
```

Afterwards we can define the filter inside of our `main.js` with the following interface: `Vue.filter('filterName', filterFunction())`. As we've abstracted the function into its own file we can import it and define it like so:

```
import Vue from 'vue';
import App from './App.vue';
import { convertDateToString } from './filters/date/date.filter';

Vue.filter('date', convertDateToString);

new Vue({
 el: '#app',
 render: h => h(App),
});
```

If you check our application again, you'll see that we get the same result as before. It is therefore important to consider where and how many times the filter will be used inside of the project. If you're using it on a specific component/instance (once) then you should place it locally; otherwise, place it globally.

Summary

In this chapter, we looked at many Vue directives and their usage. This now gives us the power to declaratively change the way our templates appear on screen, including ways to capture user input, hook into events, filter view data, and much more. This chapter should be used as a reference whenever you're looking to implement directives in a Vue.js application.

Component-based architecture is an important concept that allows us to build scalable projects that range from personal to enterprise. In the next chapter, we'll be looking at how we can create these reusable components to encapsulate pieces of functionality within our projects.

5
Secured Communication with Vue.js Components

You don't need to look far before noticing component-driven architecture in modern web applications nowadays. Development needs have changed in a short space of time with the web going from a simple document viewer to hosting complex applications with significantly large code bases. Therefore, the ability to create reusable components makes our lives as front-end developers much easier as we can encapsulate core functionality into singular blocks, reducing overall complexity, allowing for better separation of concerns, collaboration, and scalability.

In this chapter, we'll be taking the preceding concepts and applying them to our Vue applications. By the end of this chapter, you will have achieved:

- The ability to create your own Vue components
- A greater understanding of Single File Components
- The ability to create styles specific to each component
- The ability to register components both locally and globally, and an understanding of *why* to select one over the other
- The ability to communicate between parent and child components using props
- The ability to communicate *across* the application using a global Event Bus
- The ability to use slots to make your components more flexible

Let's start off by looking at *Your first Vue component*.

Your first Vue component

It turns out that we've been using components all along inside of our Vue applications! Using the `webpack-simple` template, we have support for **Single File Components (SFC)**, which is essentially just a template, script, and style tag with a `.vue` extension:

```
# Create a new Vue project
$ vue init webpack-simple vue-component-1

# Navigate to directory
$ cd vue-component-1

# Install dependencies
$ npm install

# Run application
$ npm run dev
```

As we're using the Vetur extension for Visual Studio Code, we're able to type `scaffold` and hit *Tab*, this then creates an SFC that can be used inside of our project. If we overwrite `App.vue` with an empty component, by our current definition it will look as follows:

That's it! Sort of. We've still got to add some functionality to our component, and if we were creating a new file (that is, not using the default App.vue component), register it somewhere to be used. Let's see this in action by creating a new file under src/components/FancyButton.vue:

```
<template>
 <button>
  {{buttonText}}
 </button>
</template>

<script>
export default {
 data() {
  return {
   buttonText: 'Hello World!'
  }
 }
}
</script>

<style>
 button {
  border: 1px solid black;
  padding: 10px;
 }
</style>
```

Our FancyButton component is simply a button that says 'Hello World!' and has a tiny bit of styling. Immediately, we need to be thinking about things that we can do to make this more scalable:

- Allow for an input on this component to change the button text
- As we're styling the button element (or even if we had added classes), we need a way to stop the styles leaking out into the rest of our application
- Register this component so that it can be used globally throughout the application
- Register this component so that it can be used locally within a component
- And many more!

Let's start with the easiest one, registering the component so it can be used within our application.

Registering components globally

We can create components and register them globally with the following interface: `Vue.component(name: string, options: Object<VueInstance>)`. Although it isn't required, when naming our components it's important to adhere to the naming conventions set by the W3C Custom Elements specification (`https://www.w3.org/TR/custom-elements/#valid-custom-element-name`), that is, all-lowercase and it must contain a hyphen.

Inside of our `main.js` file, let's register our `FancyButton` component by first importing it from the appropriate path:

```
import FancyButton from './components/FancyButton.vue';
```

Afterwards, we can register the component using `Vue.component`, which can be seen in bold, making the resulting code inside of `main.js` like so:

```
import Vue from 'vue';
import App from './App.vue';
import FancyButton from './components/FancyButton.vue';

Vue.component('fancy-button', FancyButton);

new Vue({
  el: '#app',
  render: h => h(App)
});
```

Tada! Our component has now been registered globally. Now... how do we use this inside of our `App.vue` component? Well, remember the tag that we specified? We just add that to the `template` like so:

```
<template>
 <fancy-button/>
</template>
```

Here's the results of our hard work (zoomed in to 500%):

Scoped styles

Great! What happens if we add another button element? As we styled the `button` element directly with CSS:

```
<template>
  <div>
    <fancy-button></fancy-button>
    <button>I'm another button!</button>
  </div>
</template>
```

If we head over to our browser we can see each of the buttons that we have created:

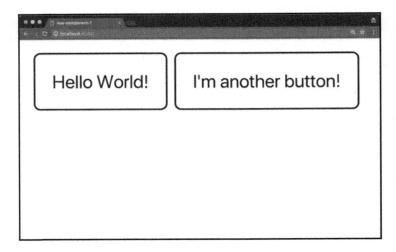

Uh oh! This other button isn't a `fancy-button`, so why is it getting the styles? Thankfully, stopping the styles from leaking outside of the component is simple, all we need to do is add the `scoped` attribute to the `style` tag:

```
<style scoped>
 button {
 border: 1px solid black;
 padding: 10px;
 }
</style>
```

The scoped attribute isn't part of Vue by default, this comes from our Webpack `vue-loader`. You'll notice that after adding this, the button styles are specific to our `fancy-button` component only. If we look at the differences between the two buttons in the following screenshot, we can see that one is merely a button and the other is styling a button with a randomly generated data attribute. This stops the browser from applying the styles to both button elements in this scenario.

When using scoped CSS within Vue, keep in mind that rules created within the component won't be accessible globally across the application:

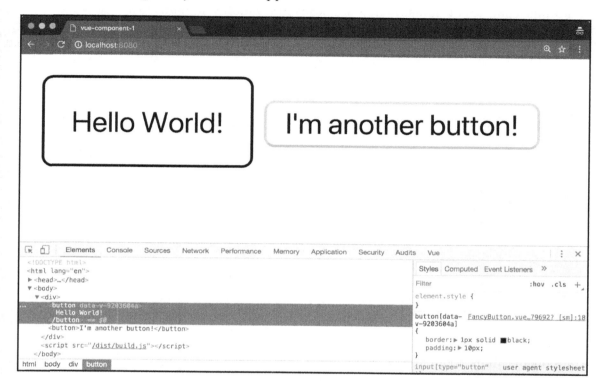

Registering a component locally

We can also register our components locally within our application. This can be done by adding it specifically to our Vue instance, for example, let's comment out the global registration within `main.js` and then navigate to `App.vue`:

```
// Vue.component('fancy-button', FancyButton);
```

Before adding any code into our app component, notice that our button has disappeared now that we're no longer globally registering it. To register this locally, we'll need to first import the component similar to how we did before and then add this to a `component` object within the instance:

```
<template>
 <div>
 <fancy-button></fancy-button>
 <button>I'm another button!</button>
 </div>
</template>

<script>
import FancyButton from './components/FancyButton.vue';

export default {
 components: {
 FancyButton
 }
}
</script>

<style>

</style>
```

Our button has now appeared on screen again. When deciding where to register your components, think about how often they may need to be used throughout the project.

Component communication

We've now got the ability to create reusable components that allow us to encapsulate functionality within our project. In order to make these components usable, we'll need to give them the ability to communicate with oneanother. The first thing we'll be looking at is one way communication with component properties (referred to as "props").

The point of component communication is to keep our features distributed, loosely coupled, and in turn make our application easier to scale. To enforce loose coupling, you should not attempt to reference parent component(s) data within the child component and it should be passed using `props` only. Let's take a look at making a property on our `FancyButton` that changes the `button` text:

```
<template>
 <button>
```

```
  {{buttonText}}
 </button>
</template>

<script>
export default {
 props: ['buttonText'],
}
</script>

<style scoped>
 button {
 border: 1px solid black;
 padding: 10px;
 }
</style>
```

Notice how we're able to bind to the buttonText value inside of our template as we've created ourselves a props array that contains string or object values for each component property. Setting this can be done with kebab case as an attribute on the component itself, this is required as HTML is case-insensitive:

```
<template>
 <fancy-button button-text="I'm set using props!"></fancy-button>
</template>
```

This gives us the following result:

Configuring property values

We can further configure our property values by instead setting them as an object. This allows us to define things such as defaults, types, validators, and so on. Let's do this with our buttonText property:

```
export default {
 props: {
  buttonText: {
   type: String,
   default: "Fancy Button!",
   required: true,
   validator: value => value.length > 3
  }
 },
}
```

Firstly, we're ensuring that we can only pass String types into this property. We can also check against other types, such as:

- Array
- Boolean
- Function
- Number
- Object
- String
- Symbol

According to web component good practices, sending primitive values to props is a good practice.

Under the hood, this is running the `instanceof` operator against the property so it could also run a check against constructor types, as seen in the following screenshot:

At the same time, we can also check for multiple types using the array syntax:

```
export default {
  props: {
    buttonText: {
      type: [String, Number, Cat],
    }
  },
}
```

Next, we're setting the default text to be `FancyButton!`, which means that by default, if this property wasn't set, it'd have that value. We've also set required equal to true, meaning that any time we create a `FancyButton` we have to include the `buttonText` property.

This is currently a contradiction in terms (that is, default value and required), but there are times where you'd want a default value where the property isn't required. Finally, we're adding a validation function to this to specify that any time we set this property, it has to have a string length greater than three.

How do we know whether a property validation has failed? In development mode, we can check our development console and we should have a corresponding error. For example, if we forget to add the `buttonText` property on our component:

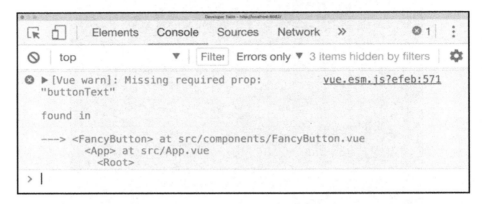

Custom events

We're making great progress. We now have a component that can accept input, be registered globally or locally, has scoped styles, validation, and more. Now we need to give it the ability to fire events back to its parent component to communicate whenever the `FancyButton` button is clicked, this is done by editing the code for the `$emit` event:

```
<template>
 <button
  @click.prevent="clicked">
  {{buttonText}}
 </button>
</template>

<script>
export default {
 props: {
  buttonText: {
   type: String,
   default: () => {
     return "Fancy Button!"
   },
   required: true,
   validator: value => value.length > 3
  }
 },
```

```
  methods: {
   clicked() {
    this.$emit('buttonClicked');
   }
  }
 }
</script>
```

In our example, we've attached the `clicked` function to the click event of the button, meaning that whenever it is selected we're emitting the `buttonClicked` event. We can then listen for this event within our `App.vue` file, where we add our element to the DOM:

```
<template>
  <fancy-button
   @buttonClicked="eventListener()"
   button-text="Click
   me!">
  </fancy-button>
</template>

<script>
import FancyButton from './components/FancyButton.vue';

export default {
  components: {
    'fancy-button': FancyButton
  },
  methods: {
    eventListener() {
      console.log("The button was clicked from the child component!");
    }
  }
}
</script>

<style>

</style>
```

Notice how at this point we're using `@buttonClicked="eventListener()"`. This uses the `v-on` event to call the `eventListener()` function any time the event is emitted, subsequently logging the message to the console. We've now demonstrated the ability to send and receive events between two components.

Sending event values

To make the event system even more powerful, we can also pass values along to our other component. Let's add an input box to our `FancyButton` component (perhaps we need to rename it or think about separating the input into its own component!):

```
<template>
 <div>
  <input type="text" v-model="message">
  <button
  @click.prevent="clicked()">
   {{buttonText}}
  </button>
 </div>
</template>

<script>
export default {
 data() {
  return {
   message: ''
  };
 },
 // Omitted
}
```

The next thing to do is pass along the message value with our `$emit` call. We can do this inside of the `clicked` method like so:

```
methods: {
 clicked() {
  this.$emit('buttonClicked', this.message);
 }
}
```

At this point, we can then capture the event as an argument to the `eventListener` function like so:

```
<template>
 <fancy-button @buttonClicked="eventListener($event)" button-text="Click me!"></fancy-button>
</template>
```

The final thing to do at this point is also match up the expected parameters for the function:

```
eventListener(message) {
  console.log(`The button was clicked from the child component with this
message: ${message}`);
}
```

We should then get the following in the console:

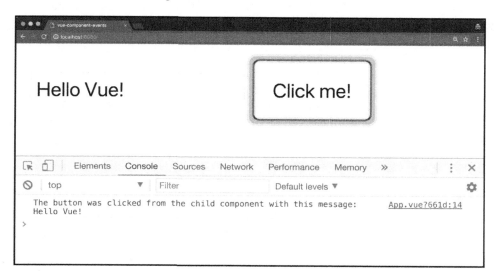

We've now got the ability to truly send events between a parent and child component, along with any data we may want to send along with it.

Event Bus

When we're looking to create an application wide events system (that is, without strictly parent to child component), we can create what's known as an Event Bus. This allows us to "pipe" all of our events through a singular Vue instance, essentially allowing for communication past just parent and child components. As well as this, it's useful for those not looking to use third-party libraries such as Vuex, or smaller projects that are not handling many actions. Let's make a new playground project to demonstrate it:

```
# Create a new Vue project
$ vue init webpack-simple vue-event-bus

# Navigate to directory
```

```
$ cd vue-event-bus

# Install dependencies
$ npm install

# Run application
$ npm run dev
```

Start off by creating an EventsBus.js inside the src folder. From here we can export a new Vue instance that we can use to emit events like before with $emit:

```
import Vue from 'vue';

export default new Vue();
```

Next, we can create our two components, ShoppingInput and ShoppingList. This will allow us to both input a new item as well as display a list of inputted items on our shopping list starting with our ShoppingInput component:

```
<template>
 <div>
  <input v-model="itemName">
  <button @click="addShoppingItem()">Add Shopping Item</button>
 </div>
</template>

<script>
import EventBus from '../EventBus';

export default {
 data() {
  return {
   itemName: ''
  }
 },
 methods: {
  addShoppingItem() {
   if(this.itemName.length > 0) {
    EventBus.$emit('addShoppingItem', this.itemName)
    this.itemName = "";
   }
  }
 },
}
</script>
```

The key take away from this component is that we're now importing EventBus and using $emit instead of using this, changing our application's event system from being component-based to application-based. We can then watch for changes (and the subsequent values) from any component we want using $on. Let's look at this with our next component, ShoppingList:

```
<template>
 <div>
  <ul>
   <li v-for="item in shoppingList" :key="item">
    {{item}}
   </li>
  </ul>
 </div>
</template>

<script>
import EventBus from '../EventBus';
export default {
 props: ['shoppingList'],
 created() {
  EventBus.$on('addShoppingItem', (item) => {
   console.log(`There was an item added! ${item}`);
  })
 }
}
</script>
```

Looking at our ShoppingList component we can see the use of $on, this allows us to listen for the event named addShoppingItem (the same event name as we emitted, or any other event you're looking to listen for). This returns the item, which we're then able to log out to the console or do anything else at this point.

We can put this all together inside of our App.vue:

```
<template>
 <div>
  <shopping-input/>
  <shopping-list :shoppingList="shoppingList"/>
 </div>
</template>

<script>
import ShoppingInput from './components/ShoppingInput';
import ShoppingList from './components/ShoppingList';
import EventBus from './EventBus';
```

```
export default {
 components: {
  ShoppingInput,
  ShoppingList
 },
 data() {
  return {
   shoppingList: []
  }
 },
 created() {
  EventBus.$on('addShoppingItem', (itemName) => {
   this.shoppingList.push(itemName);
  })
 },
}
```

We're defining both of our components, and listening for the addShoppingItem event inside of our created lifecycle hook. Just as before, we get the itemName, which we can then add to our array. We can pass the array through to another component as a prop, such as the ShoppingList to be rendered on screen.

Finally, if we wanted to stop listening to events (either entirely or per event) we can use $off. Inside of App.vue, let's make a new button that shows this further:

```
<button @click="stopListening()">Stop listening</button>
```

Then we can create the stopListening method like so:

```
methods: {
 stopListening() {
  EventBus.$off('addShoppingItem')
 }
},
```

If we wanted to stop listening to all events, we could simply use:

```
EventBus.$off();
```

At this point, we've now created an events system that would allow us to communicate with any of our components regardless of the parent/child relationship. We're able to send events and listen to them via the EventBus, giving us a lot more flexibility with our component data.

Slots

When we're composing our components, we should consider how they'll be used by ourselves and our team. Using slots allows us to dynamically add elements to the component with varying behavior. Let's see this in action by making a new playground project:

```
# Create a new Vue project
$ vue init webpack-simple vue-slots

# Navigate to directory
$ cd vue-slots

# Install dependencies
$ npm install

# Run application
$ npm run dev
```

We can then go ahead and create a new component named `Message` (`src/components/Message.vue`). We can then add something specific to this component (such as the following h1) as well as a `slot` tag that we can use to inject content from elsewhere:

```
<template>
 <div>
   <h1>I'm part of the Message component!</h1>
   <slot></slot>
 </div>
</template>

<script>
export default {}
</script>
```

If we then registered our component inside of `App.vue` and placed it inside of our template, we'd be able to add content inside of the `component` tag like so:

```
<template>
 <div id="app">
   <message>
     <h2>What are you doing today?</h2>
   </message>
   <message>
     <h2>Learning about Slots in Vue.</h2>
   </message>
```

```
    </div>
  </template>

  <script>
  import Message from './components/Message';

  export default {
   components: {
    Message
   }
  }
  </script>
```

At this point, everything inside the `message` tag is being placed inside of the `slot` within our `Message` component:

Notice how we're seeing **I'm part of the Message component!** with each declaration of the `Message` component, this shows that even though we're injecting content into this space, we can still show template information specific to the component each time.

Defaults

Whilst we're able to add content into the slots, we may want to add default content that shows when we don't add anything ourselves. This means we don't have to add content every time, and if we want to, we can override it in that circumstance.

How do we add default behavior to our slots? That's quite simple! All we need to do is add our element(s) in between the `slot` tag like this:

```
<template>
 <div>
  <h1>I'm part of the Message component!</h1>
  <slot>
   <h2>I'm a default heading that appears <em>only</em> when no slots
   have been passed into this component</h2>
  </slot>
 </div>
</template>
```

If we therefore add another `message` element, but this time without any markup inside, we'd get the following:

```
<template>
 <div id="app">
  <message>
   <h2>What are you doing today?</h2>
  </message>
  <message>
   <h2>Learning about Slots in Vue.</h2>
  </message>
  <message></message>
 </div>
</template>
```

Now if we head to our browser we can see that our messages display as expected like so:

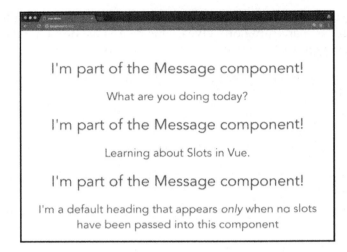

Named slots

We can also take this a step further with named slots. Let's say our `message` component wanted both a `date` and `messageText` input, one of which is a slot and the other a property of the component. Our use case for this would be that perhaps we want to display the date differently, add varying bits of information, or not even show it at all.

Our message component becomes:

```
<template>
 <div>
  <slot name="date"></slot>
  <h1>{{messageText}}</h1>
 </div>
</template>

<script>
export default {
 props: ['messageText']
}
</script>
```

Take note of the `name="date"` attribute on our `slot` tag. This allows us to dynamically place our content at runtime in the correct locations. We can then build out a small chat system to show this in action, let's ensure we have `moment` installed in our project prior to continuing:

```
$ npm install moment --save
```

You may remember using `moment` in `Chapter 4`, *Vue.js Directives*, we'll also be reusing the `Date` pipe that we created earlier. Let's upgrade our `App.vue` to contain the following:

```
<template>
 <div id="app">

  <input type="text" v-model="message">
  <button @click="sendMessage()">+</button>

  <message v-for="message in messageList" :message-text="message.text"
:key="message">
   <h2 slot="date">{{ message.date | date }}</h2>
  </message>
 </div>
</template>

<script>
import moment from 'moment';
import Message from './components/Message';

const convertDateToString = value =>
moment(String(value)).format('MM/DD/YYYY');

export default {
 data() {
  return {
   message: '',
   messageList: []
  }
 },
 methods: {
  sendMessage() {
   if ( this.message.length > 0 ) {
    this.messageList.push({ date: new Date(), text: this.message });
    this.message = ""
   }
  }
 },
 components: {
  Message
```

```
  },
  filters: {
   date: convertDateToString
  }
 }
</script>
```

What's happening here? Inside of our template we're iterating over our `messageList` and creating a new message component each time a new message is added. Inside of the component tag we're expecting the `messageText` to appear (as we're passing it as a prop and the markup is defined inside the Message component), but we're also dynamically adding the date using a `slot`:

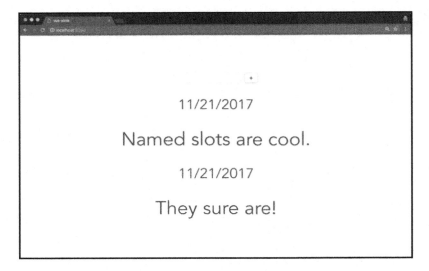

What happens if we remove `slot="date"` from our h2? Does the date still show? Nope. This is because when we only use named slots, there are no other places for the slot to be added. It would only appear if we changed our `Message` component to take in an unnamed slot like so:

```
<template>
 <div>
  <slot name="date"></slot>
  <slot></slot>
  <h1>{{messageText}}</h1>
 </div>
</template>
```

Summary

This chapter has given us the power to create reusable components that can communicate with one another. We've looked at how we can register components globally throughout the project, or locally to a specific instance, giving us flexibility and appropriate separation of concerns. We've seen just how powerful this can be with examples that range from the addition of simple properties to complex validations and defaults.

In the next chapter, we're going to be investigating how we can create **better UI.** We'll be looking more at directives such as v-model in the context of forms, animations, and validation.

6
Creating Better UI

Transitions and animations are great ways of creating a better user experience within our applications. As there's so many different options and use cases, they can make or break the feel of an application if under or overused. We'll be looking at this concept further within this chapter.

We'll also be looking at form validation with a third-party library named `Vuelidate`. This will allow us to create forms that scale with the size of our application. We'll also gain the power to change the UI depending on form state, as well as display helpful validation messages to assist the user.

Finally, we'll look at how we can use the `render` function and JSX to compose the user interface with Vue. While this is not perfect for every scenario, there are times where you'd want to take full advantage of JavaScript within your templates, as well as create smart/presentational components with the Functional Component model.

By the end of this chapter, you will have:

- Learned about CSS animations
- Created your own CSS animations
- Used `Animate.css` to create interactive UI with little work
- Investigated and created your own Vue transitions
- Taken advantage of `Vuelidate` to validate forms within Vue
- Used the `render` function as an alternative to template-driven UI
- Used JSX to compose UI similar to React

Let's start off by understanding why we should care about animation and transitions inside our project(s).

Animations

Animations can be used to draw focus to specific UI elements and to improve the overall experience for the user by bringing it to life. Animations should be used when there is no clear start state and end state. An animation can be set to play automatically or it can be triggered by user interaction.

CSS animations

CSS animations are not only a powerful tool, but they are also easy to maintain with little knowledge needed in order to use them within a project.

Adding them to an interface can be an intuitive method of capturing a user's attention and they can also be used in pointing a user to a specific element with ease. The animations can be tailored and customized, making them ideal for plenty of use cases within a variety of projects.

Before we dig deep into Vue transitions and other animated possibilities, we should have an understanding of how to do basic CSS3 animations. Let's create a simple project that looks at this in more detail:

```
# Create a new Vue project
$ vue init webpack-simple vue-css-animations

# Navigate to directory
$ cd vue-css-animations

# Install dependencies
$ npm install

# Run application
$ npm run dev
```

Inside App.vue we can first create the following styles:

```
<style>
button {
 background-color: transparent;
 padding: 5px;
 border: 1px solid black;
}

h1 {
```

```
 opacity: 0;
}

@keyframes fade {
 from { opacity: 0; }
 to { opacity: 1; }
}

.animated {
 animation: fade 1s;
 opacity: 1;
}
</style>
```

As you can see, nothing too out of the ordinary. We're declaring the CSS animation with @keyframes named fade, essentially giving CSS two states that we want our element to be in - opacity: 1 and opacity: 0. It says nothing about how long or whether these keyframes are repeated; this is all done in the animated class. We're applying the fade keyframes for 1s whenever we add the class to an element; at the same time, we're adding opacity: 1 to ensure that it doesn't disappear after the animation has ended.

We can put this together by taking advantage of v-bind:class to dynamically add/remove the class depending on the value of toggle:

```
<template>
 <div id="app">
  <h1 v-bind:class="{ animated: toggle }">I fade in!</h1>
  <button @click="toggle = !toggle">Toggle Heading</button>
 </div>
</template>

<script>
export default {
 data () {
  return {
   toggle: false
  }
 }
}
</script>
```

Cool. We now have the ability to fade in a heading based on a `Boolean` value. But what if we could do it better? In this particular circumstance, we could have used a transition to achieve similar results. Prior to looking at transitions in more detail, let's look at other ways we can use CSS animations inside our project.

Animate.css

`Animate.css` is a great way of implementing different types of animation easily into your project. It's an open source CSS library created by Daniel Eden (`https://daneden.me/`) and it gives us access to "plug and play" CSS animations.

Prior to adding it to any project, head over to `https://daneden.github.io/animate.css/` and preview the different animation styles. There are a lot of different animations to choose from, with each offering a different default animation. These can be further customized and we'll talk more about that later on in the section.

Go ahead and create a playground project by running the following in our Terminal:

```
Create a new Vue project
$ vue init webpack-simple vue-animate-css

# Navigate to directory
$ cd vue-animate-css

# Install dependencies
$ npm install

# Run application
$ npm run dev
```

Once the project is set up, go ahead and open it up in the editor of your choice and head to the `index.html` file. Inside the `<head>` tag, add the following stylesheet:

```
<link rel="stylesheet"
href="https://cdnjs.cloudflare.com/ajax/libs/animate.css/3.5.2/animate.min.
css">
```

This is the stylesheet reference needed for `Animate.css` to work on the project.

Using Animate.css

Now that we have `Animate.css` inside the project, we can change our `App.vue` to have a `template` with the following:

```
<template>
 <h1 class="animated fadeIn">Hello Vue!</h1>
</template>
```

Prior to adding any animations, we first need to add the animated class. Next, we can select any animation from the `Animate.css` library; we've chosen `fadeIn` for this example. This can then be switched out for other animations such as `bounceInLeft`, `shake`, `rubberBand`, and many more!

We could take our previous example, and turn this into a bound class value based on a Boolean - but transitions may be more exciting to look at.

Transitions

Transitions work by starting off in one particular state and then transitioning into another state and interpolating the values in-between. A transition can't have multiple steps involved in an animation. Imagine a pair of curtains going from open to closed: the first state would be the open position, while the second state would be the closed position.

Vue has its own tags for dealing with transitions, known as `<transition>` and `<transition-group>`. These tags are customizable and can be easily used with JavaScript and CSS. There do not necessarily need to be `transition` tags to make transitions work, as you simply bind the state variable to a visible property, but the tags typically offer more control and potentially better results.

Let's take the `toggle` example that we had before and create a version that uses `transition`:

```
<template>
 <div id="app">
  <transition name="fadeIn"
  enter-active-class="animated fadeIn"
  leave-active-class="animated fadeOut">
   <h1 v-if="toggle">I fade in and out!</h1>
```

```
      </transition>
      <button @click="toggle = !toggle">Toggle Heading</button>
    </div>
  </template>

  <script>
  export default {
   data () {
    return {
     toggle: false
    }
   }
  }
  </script>
```

Let's take a look at the moving parts in more detail.

We're surrounding the element inside a `<transition>` tag, which is applied to `enter-active-class` of `animated fadeIn` whenever `<h1>` enters the DOM. This is triggered with the `v-if` directive as the `toggle` variable is initially set to `false`. Clicking the button toggles our Boolean, triggering the transition and applying the appropriate CSS class.

Transition states

Every enter/leave transition applies up to six classes, which are made up of transitions upon entering the scene, during, and leaving the scene. Set one (`v-enter-*`) refers to Transitions initially entering and then moving out, while set two (`v-leave-*`) refers to ending transitions entering and then moving out:

Name	Description
v-enter	This is the very starting state for enter. It is removed one frame after the element is inserted.
v-enter-active	`enter-active` is `enter`'s active state. It is active for the entirety of the active phase and is only removed once the transitions or animations have come to an end. This state also manages further instructions such as delays, duration, and so on.
v-enter-to	This is the last state for enter, added one frame after the element is inserted, which is the same time `v-enter` is removed. `Enter-to` is then removed once the transition/animation ends.

v-leave	This is the starting state for leave. Removed after one frame once a leave transition is triggered to take place.
v-leave-active	leave-active is leave's active state. It is active for the entirety of the leaving phase and is only removed once the transition or animation have come to an end.
v-leave-to	The last state for leave, added one frame after a leave is triggered, which is the same time v-leave is removed. Leave-to is then removed when the transition/animation ends.

Each enter and leave transition features a prefix, which in the table is shown as the default value of v because the transition itself has no name. When adding the enter or leave transitions into a project, ideally proper naming conventions should apply to act as unique identifiers. This can help if you plan on using multiple transitions within a project and can be done through a simple assignment operation:

```
<transition name="my-transition">
```

Form validation

Throughout the book, we've looked at various different ways that we can capture user input with the likes of v-model. We'll be using a third-party library named **Vuelidate** to perform model validation depending on a particular ruleset. Let's create a playground project by running the following in your Terminal:

```
# Create a new Vue project
$ vue init webpack-simple vue-validation

# Navigate to directory
$ cd vue-validation

# Install dependencies
$ npm install

# Install Vuelidate
$ npm install vuelidate

# Run application
$ npm run dev
```

What is Vuelidate?

`Vuelidate` is an open source, lightweight library that helps us perform model validation with a variety of validation contexts. Validation can be functionally composed and it also works well with other libraries such as `Moment`, `Vuex`, and more. As we've installed it in our project with `npm install vuelidate`, we now need to register it as a plugin within `main.js`:

```
import Vue from 'vue';
import Vuelidate from 'vuelidate';
import App from './App.vue';

Vue.use(Vuelidate);

new Vue({
  el: '#app',
  validations: {},
  render: h => h(App),
});
```

Adding the empty validations object to our main Vue instance bootstraps Vuelidate's `$v` throughout the project. This then allows us to use the `$v` object to gain information about the current state of our form within our Vue instance across all components.

Using Vuelidate

Let's create a basic form that allows us to input a `firstName`, `lastName`, `email`, and `password`. This will allow us to add validation rules with `Vuelidate` and visualize them on screen:

```
<template>
  <div>
    <form class="form" @submit.prevent="onSubmit">
      <div class="input">
        <label for="email">Email</label>
        <input
        type="email"
        id="email"
        v-model.trim="email">
      </div>
      <div class="input">
        <label for="firstName">First Name</label>
        <input
        type="text"
```

```
          id="firstName"
          v-model.trim="firstName">
      </div>
      <div class="input">
        <label for="lastName">Last Name</label>
        <input
        type="text"
        id="lastName"
        v-model.trim="lastName">
      </div>
      <div class="input">
        <label for="password">Password</label>
        <input
        type="password"
        id="password"
        v-model.trim="password">
      </div>
      <button type="submit">Submit</button>
    </form>
  </div>
</template>
<script>
export default {
  data() {
    return {
      email: '',
      password: '',
      firstName: '',
      lastName: '',
    };
  },
  methods: {
    onSubmit(){
    }
  },
}
</script>
```

There's a lot going on here, so let's break it down step by step:

1. We're creating a new form with the @submit.prevent directive so that the page doesn't reload when the form is submitted, which is the same as calling the submit on this form and having preventDefault on the event

2. Next, we're adding v-model.trim to each form input element so that we trim any white space and capture the input as a variable

3. We're defining these variables inside of our data function so that they're reactive
4. The submit button is defined with the type="submit" so that when it's clicked the form's submit function is ran
5. We're stubbing out a blank onSubmit function, which we'll be creating soon

Now we need to add the @input event and call the touch event on each one of our input elements, binding to the data property v-model, and providing validation to the field like so:

```
<div class="input">
  <label for="email">Email</label>
  <input
  type="email"
  id="email"
  @input="$v.email.$touch()"
  v-model.trim="email">
</div>
<div class="input">
  <label for="firstName">First Name</label>
  <input
  type="text"
  id="firstName"
  v-model.trim="firstName"
  @input="$v.firstName.$touch()">
</div>
<div class="input">
  <label for="lastName">Last Name</label>
  <input
  type="text"
  id="lastName"
  v-model.trim="lastName"
  @input="$v.lastName.$touch()">
</div>
<div class="input">
  <label for="password">Password</label>
  <input
  type="password"
  id="password"
  v-model.trim="password"
  @input="$v.password.$touch()">
</div>
```

We can then add the validations to our Vue instance by importing them from Vuelidate and adding a validations object that corresponds to the form elements.

`Vuelidate` will bind the same name set here with our `data` variable like so:

```
import { required, email } from 'vuelidate/lib/validators';

export default {
// Omitted
  validations: {
    email: {
      required,
      email,
    },
    firstName: {
      required,
    },
    lastName: {
      required,
    },
    password: {
      required,
    }
  },
}
```

We're simply importing the required email validators and applying them to each model item. This essentially makes sure that all of our items are required and that the email input matches an email regular expression. We can then visualize the current state of the form and each field by adding the following:

```
<div class="validators">
 <pre>{{$v}}</pre>
</div>
```

We can then add some styling to show the validation on the right and the form on the left:

```
<style>
.form {
 display: inline-block;
 text-align: center;
 width: 49%;
}
.validators {
 display: inline-block;
 width: 49%;
 text-align: center;
 vertical-align: top;
}
.input {
```

```
   padding: 5px;
}
</style>
```

If everything has gone as planned, we should get the following result:

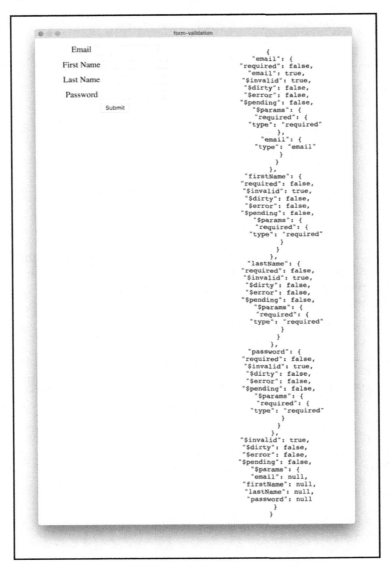

Displaying form errors

We can use the $invalid Boolean inside of the $v.model_name object (where model_name is equal to email, firstName, lastName, or password) to display messages or change the look and feel of our form field(s). Let's start off by adding a new class named error that adds a red border around the input field:

```
<style>
input:focus {
  outline: none;
}
.error {
  border: 1px solid red;
}
</style>
```

We can then conditionally apply this class whenever the field is invalid and touched using v-bind:class:

```
<div class="input">
  <label for="email">Email</label>
  <input
  :class="{ error: $v.email.$error }"
  type="email"
  id="email"
  @input="$v.email.$touch()"
  v-model.trim="email">
</div>
<div class="input">
  <label for="firstName">First Name</label>
  <input
  :class="{ error: $v.firstName.$error }"
  type="text"
  id="firstName"
  v-model.trim="firstName"
  @input="$v.firstName.$touch()">
</div>
<div class="input">
  <label for="lastName">Last Name</label>
  <input
  :class="{ error: $v.lastName.$error}"
  type="text"
  id="lastName"
  v-model.trim="lastName"
  @input="$v.lastName.$touch()">
</div>
<div class="input">
```

```
    <label for="password">Password</label>
    <input
    :class="{ error: $v.password.$error }"
    type="password"
    id="password"
    v-model.trim="password"
    @input="$v.password.$touch()">
  </div>
```

This then gives us the following results whenever the field is invalid or valid:

Subsequently, we can then display an error message if this is the case. This can be done in numerous ways depending on the type of message you want to show. Let's use the `email` input as an example, and show an error message when the `email` field has an invalid email address:

```
<div class="input">
  <label for="email">Email</label>
  <input
  :class="{ error: $v.email.$error }"
  type="email"
  id="email"
  @input="$v.email.$touch()"
  v-model.trim="email">

  <p class="error-message" v-if="!$v.email.email">Please enter a valid
email address</p>
</div>

// Omitted
<style>
.error-message {
 color: red;
}
</style>
```

As we can see from the representation of our $v object, the email Boolean is true when the field has a valid email address, and if not, is false. While this checks to see if email is correct, it doesn't check to see whether the field is empty. Let's add another error message that checks this based on the `required` validator:

```
<p class="error-message" v-if="!$v.email.email">Please enter a valid email
address.</p>
<p class="error-message" v-if="!$v.email.required">Email must not be
empty.</p>
```

If we wanted to, we could even take this a step further and create our own wrapper component that would render the various error messages of each field. Let's fill in the rest of our error messages along with a check to see whether the form element has been touched (is $dirty):

```
<div class="input">
  <label for="email">Email</label>
  <input
  :class="{ error: $v.email.$error }"
  type="email"
  id="email"
  @input="$v.email.$touch()"
  v-model.trim="email">

  <div v-if="$v.email.$dirty">
    <p class="error-message" v-if="!$v.email.email">Please enter a
    valid email address.</p>
    <p class="error-message" v-if="!$v.email.required">Email must not
    be empty.</p>
  </div>

</div>
<div class="input">
  <label for="firstName">First Name</label>
  <input
  :class="{ error: $v.firstName.$error }"
  type="text"
  id="firstName"
  v-model.trim="firstName"
  @input="$v.firstName.$touch()">
  <div v-if="$v.firstName.$dirty">
    <p class="error-message" v-if="!$v.firstName.required">First Name
  must not be empty.</p>
  </div>
</div>
<div class="input">
  <label for="lastName">Last Name</label>
```

```
<input
:class="{ error: $v.lastName.$error}"
type="text"
id="lastName"
v-model.trim="lastName"
@input="$v.lastName.$touch()">

<div v-if="$v.lastName.$dirty">
  <p class="error-message" v-if="!$v.lastName.required">Last Name
 must not be empty.</p>
</div>
</div>
<div class="input">
  <label for="password">Password</label>
  <input
  :class="{ error: $v.password.$error }"
  type="password"
  id="password"
  v-model.trim="password"
  @input="$v.password.$touch()">

  <div v-if="$v.password.$dirty">
    <p class="error-message" v-if="!$v.password.required">Password must
not be empty.</p>
  </div>
</div>
```

Password validation

When creating user accounts, passwords tend to be entered twice and conform to a minimum length. Let's add another field and some more validation rules to enforce this:

```
import { required, email, minLength, sameAs } from
'vuelidate/lib/validators';

export default {
 // Omitted
  data() {
    return {
      email: '',
      password: '',
      repeatPassword: '',
      firstName: '',
      lastName: '',
    };
  },
```

```
validations: {
  email: {
    required,
    email,
  },
  firstName: {
    required,
  },
  lastName: {
    required,
  },
  password: {
    required,
    minLength: minLength(6),
  },
  repeatPassword: {
    required,
    minLength: minLength(6),
    sameAsPassword: sameAs('password'),
  },
},
}
```

We've done the following:

1. Added the `repeatPassword` field to our data object so that it can hold the repeated password
2. Imported both the `minLength` and `sameAs` validators from `Vuelidate`
3. Added the `minLength` of 6 characters to the `password` validator
4. Added the `sameAs` validator to enforce the fact that `repeatPassword` should follow the same validation rules as `password`

As we now have appropriate password validation, we can add the new field and display any error messages:

```
<div class="input">
<label for="email">Email</label>
<input
:class="{ error: $v.email.$error }"
type="email"
id="email"
@input="$v.email.$touch()"
v-model.trim="email">

<div v-if="$v.email.$dirty">
<p class="error-message" v-if="!$v.email.email">Please enter a valid email
```

```
address.</p>
 <p class="error-message" v-if="!$v.email.required">Email must not be
empty.</p>
 </div>

</div>
<div class="input">
 <label for="firstName">First Name</label>
 <input
 :class="{ error: $v.firstName.$error }"
 type="text"
 id="firstName"
 v-model.trim="firstName"
 @input="$v.firstName.$touch()">

 <div v-if="$v.firstName.$dirty">
 <p class="error-message" v-if="!$v.firstName.required">First Name must not
be empty.</p>
 </div>
</div>
<div class="input">
 <label for="lastName">Last Name</label>
 <input
 :class="{ error: $v.lastName.$error}"
 type="text"
 id="lastName"
 v-model.trim="lastName"
 @input="$v.lastName.$touch()">

 <div v-if="$v.lastName.$dirty">
 <p class="error-message" v-if="!$v.lastName.required">Last Name must not
be empty.</p>
 </div>
</div>
<div class="input">
 <label for="password">Password</label>
 <input
 :class="{ error: $v.password.$error }"
 type="password"
 id="password"
 v-model.trim="password"
 @input="$v.password.$touch()">

 <div v-if="$v.password.$dirty">
 <p class="error-message" v-if="!$v.password.required">Password must not be
empty.</p>
 </div>
</div>
```

```
<div class="input">
 <label for="repeatPassword">Repeat Password</label>
 <input
 :class="{ error: $v.repeatPassword.$error }"
 type="password"
 id="repeatPassword"
 v-model.trim="repeatPassword"
 @input="$v.repeatPassword.$touch()">

 <div v-if="$v.repeatPassword.$dirty">
 <p class="error-message" v-
if="!$v.repeatPassword.sameAsPassword">Passwords must be identical.</p>

 <p class="error-message" v-if="!$v.repeatPassword.required">Password must
not be empty.</p>
 </div>
</div>
```

Form submission

Next, we can disable our Submit button if the form is not valid:

```
<button :disabled="$v.$invalid" type="submit">Submit</button>
```

We can also get this value inside of our JavaScript with this.$v.$invalid. Here's an example of how we can check to see whether the form is invalid and then create a user object based on our form elements:

```
methods: {
  onSubmit() {
    if(!this.$v.$invalid) {
      const user = {
        email: this.email,
        firstName: this.firstName,
        lastName: this.lastName,
        password: this.password,
        repeatPassword: this.repeatPassword
      }

      // Submit the object to an API of sorts
    }
  },
},
```

If you'd like to use your data in this fashion, you may prefer to set up your data object like so:

```
data() {
  return {
    user: {
      email: '',
      password: '',
      repeatPassword: '',
      firstName: '',
      lastName: '',
    }
  };
},
```

We have now created a form with appropriate validation!

Render/functional components

We're going to take a detour and pivot away from validation and animations to consider the use of functional components and render functions to improve application performance. You may also hear these being referred to as "presentational components" as they're stateless and only receive data as an input prop.

So far, we've only declared the markup for our components with the `template` tag, but it's also possible to use the `render` function (as seen in `src/main.js`):

```
import Vue from 'vue'
import App from './App.vue'

new Vue({
  el: '#app',
  render: h => h(App)
})
```

The `h` comes from hyperscript that allows us to create/describe DOM nodes with our JavaScript. In the `render` function, we're simply rendering the `App` component and in the future, we'll be looking at this in more detail. Vue creates a Virtual DOM to make working with the actual DOM much simpler (as well as for improved performance when dealing with a vast amount of elements).

Rendering elements

We can replace our App.vue component with the following object that takes a render object and hyperscript instead of using template:

```
<script>
export default {
 render(h) {
  return h('h1', 'Hello render!')
 }
}
</script>
```

This then renders a new h1 tag with the text node of 'Hello render!' and this is then known as a **VNode (Virtual Node)** and the plural **VNodes (Virtual DOM Nodes)**, which describes the entire tree. Let's now look at how we can display a list of items inside of a ul:

```
render(h){
  h('ul', [
    h('li', 'Evan You'),
    h('li', 'Edd Yerburgh'),
    h('li', 'Paul Halliday')
  ])
}
```

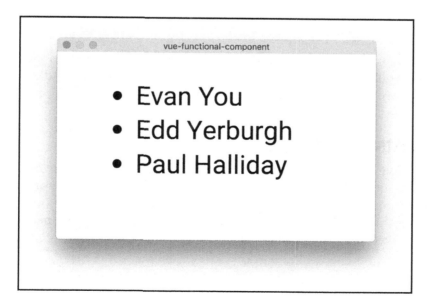

It's important to realize that we can only render one root node with hyperscript. This restriction is the same for our template, so it's expected that we wrap our items inside of a div like so:

```
render(h) {
 return h('div', [
  h('ul', [
   h('li', 'Evan You'),
   h('li', 'Edd Yerburgh'),
   h('li', 'Paul Halliday')
  ])
 ])
}
```

Attributes

We can also pass style elements and a variety of other attributes to our rendered items. Here's an example that uses the style object to change the color of each item red:

```
h('div', [
 h('ul', { style: { color: 'red' } }, [
  h('li', 'Evan You'),
  h('li', 'Edd Yerburgh'),
  h('li', 'Paul Halliday')
 ])
])
```

As you can imagine, we can add as many style attributes as we want, as well as extra options that we would expect, such as props, directives, on (click handlers), and so on. Let's look at how we can map over elements to render a component with props.

Components and props

Let's create ourselves a ListItem component under components/ListItem.vue with one prop, name. We'll render this component in place of our li and map over an array that contains various names. Notice how we're also adding the functional: true option to our Vue instance; this tells Vue that this is purely a presentational component and it will not have any state of its own:

```
<script>
export default {
 props: ['name'],
 functional: true
```

```
  }
</script>
```

With our `render` function, `h` is often also referred to as `createElement`, and because we're in the JavaScript context, we're able to take advantage of array operators such as `map`, `filter`, `reduce`, and so on. Let's replace the static names for dynamically generated components with `map`:

```
import ListItem from './components/ListItem.vue';

export default {
  data() {
    return {
     names: ['Evan You', 'Edd Yerburgh', 'Paul Halliday']
    }
  },
  render(createElement) {
   return createElement('div', [
    createElement('ul',
     this.names.map(name =>
      createElement(ListItem,
       {props: { name: name } })
      ))
    ])
  }
}
```

The final thing we need to do is add a `render` function to our component. As a second parameter, we're able to gain access to the context object, which allows us to access `options` such as our `props`. For this example, we'll assume that the `name` prop is always present and isn't `null` or `undefined`:

```
export default {
  props: ['name'],
  functional: true,
  render(createElement, context) {
   return createElement('li', context.props.name)
  }
}
```

Once again, we now have a list of elements that includes items passed as a `prop`:

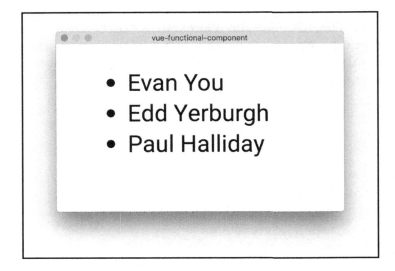

JSX

Although this is a great thought exercise, templates are superior in most cases. There may be times where you want to use the render function inside of your components and, in these circumstances, it may be simpler to use JSX.

Let's add the babel plugin for JSX into our project by running the following in our Terminal:

```
$ npm i -D babel-helper-vue-jsx-merge-props babel-plugin-syntax-jsx babel-plugin-transform-vue-jsx
```

We can then update our `.babelrc` to use the new plugin:

```
{
  "presets": [
  ["env", { "modules": false }],
  "stage-3"
  ],
  "plugins": ["transform-vue-jsx"]
}
```

This allows us to rewrite our `render` function to take advantage of a simpler syntax:

```
render(h) {
  return (
    <div>
     <ul>
       { this.names.map(name => <ListItem name={name} />) }
     </ul>
    </div>
  )
}
```

This is much more declarative and is also easier to maintain. Under the hood, it's being transpiled down to the previous `hyperscript` format with Babel.

Summary

In this chapter, we learned how to take advantage of CSS animations and transitions within our Vue projects. This allows us to make the user experience more fluid and improve the look and feel of our applications.

We also learned about how we can construct our UI with the `render` method; this involved looking at creating VNodes with HyperScript and then using JSX for cleaner abstraction. While you may not want to use JSX in your project, you may find it more comfortable if you come from a React background.

7
HTTP and WebSocket Communication

In this chapter, we'll be looking at how we can interface with our server-side APIs using HTTP. We will create an application using our own offline API with HTTP GET, POST, PUT, PATCH, and DELETE. As well as this, we'll be creating an in-memory, real-time chat application that takes advantage of WebSockets with the Socket.io library.

By the end of this chapter, you will know how to:

- Create a mock database APIs with json-server
- Create HTTP requests with Axios
- Use WebSockets and Socket.io for real-time communication across clients

HTTP

Let's start off by creating a new Vue.js project that we can use as a playground project. Type the following in your Terminal:

```
# Create a new Vue project
$ vue init webpack-simple vue-http

# Navigate to directory
$ cd vue-http
```

```
# Install dependencies
$ npm install

# Run application
$ npm run dev
```

There are many ways to create HTTP requests within JavaScript. We'll be using the Axios library to use a simplified promise-based approach within our project. Let's install it by typing the following in our Terminal:

```
# Install Axios to our project
$ npm install axios --save
```

We now have the ability to create HTTP requests; we just need an API to point Axios towards. Let's create a mock API.

Installing JSON server

In order to create a mock API, we can use the json-server library. This allows us to get up-and-running globally quickly by just creating a db.json file inside of our project. It effectively creates a GET, POST, PUT, PATCH, and DELETE API and stores the data in a file, appended to our original JSON file.

We can install it by running the following in our Terminal:

```
# Install the json-server module globally
$ npm install json-server -g
```

As we've added the -g flag, we'll be able to access the json-server module globally throughout our Terminal.

The next thing we need to do is create our db.json file inside the root of our project. Be as creative as you want with your dataset; we just simply have a list of courses that we may or may not be interested in:

```
{
  "courses": [
    {
      "id": 1,
      "name": "Vue.js Design Patterns"
    },
    {
      "id": 2,
      "name": "Angular: From Beginner to Advanced"
```

```
    },
    {
      "id": 3,
      "name": "Cross Platform Native Applications with Fuse"
    }
  ]
}
```

We can then run our database by running the following in the Terminal:

```
# Run the database based on our db.json file
$ json-server db.json --watch
```

If we've done everything successfully, we should then be able to access our database at `http://localhost:3000`, as seen by the following success message:

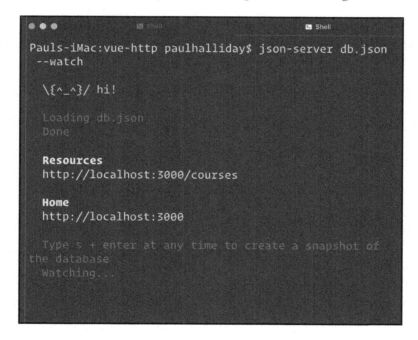

Awesome. We're all set up and now we can get a list of courses.

HTTP GET

The first thing we need to do is import `Axios` into our `App.vue` component. We can also set a `ROOT_URL` in this instance as we'll only be looking for the `/courses` endpoint:

```
<script>
import axios from 'axios'
export default {
  data() {
    return {
      ROOT_URL: 'http://localhost:3000/courses',
      courses: []
    }
  }
}
</script>
```

This then gives us the ability to hook into a lifecycle hook such as `created()` and call a method that requests the courses from our API:

```
export default {
  data() {
    return {
      ROOT_URL: 'http://localhost:3000/courses',
      courses: []
    }
  },
  created() {
    this.getCourseList();
  },
  methods: {
    getCourseList() {
      axios
        .get(this.ROOT_URL)
        .then(response => {
          this.courses = response.data;
        })
        .catch(error => console.log(error));
    }
  }
}
```

What's happening here? We're calling the `getCoursesList` function, which makes an HTTP `GET` request to our `http://localhost:3000/courses` endpoint. This then either sets the courses array equal to the data (that is, everything inside of our `db.json`) or merely logs out an error if there was one.

We can then display this on screen using the v- for directive:

```
<template>
  <div class="course-list">
    <h1>Courses</h1>
    <div v-for="course in courses" v-bind:key="course.id">
      <p>
        {{course.name}}
      </p>
    </div>
  </div>
</template>
```

Together with a little bit of styling, we get:

```
<style>
.course-list {
  background-color: rebeccapurple;
  padding: 10px;
  width: 50%;
  text-align: center;
  margin: 0 auto;
  color: white;
}
</style>
```

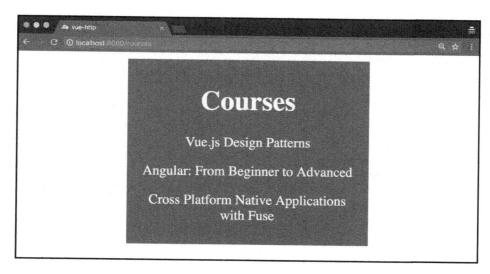

Let's move on to HTTP POST!

HTTP POST

We can add an input box and `button` following the `courseName div`, allowing the user to input a new course to their learning list:

```
<div>
 <input type="text" v-model="courseName" placeholder="Course name">
 <button @click="addCourse(courseName)">Add</button>
</div>
```

This requires us to add the `courseName` variable to our `data` object:

```
data() {
 return {
  ROOT_URL: 'http://localhost:3000/courses/',
  courses: [],
  courseName: '',
 };
},
```

We can then create a similar method named `addCourse` that takes the `courseName` as a parameter:

```
methods: {
// Omitted
 addCourse(name) {
  axios
   .post(this.ROOT_URL, { name })
   .then(response => {
     this.courses.push(response.data);
     this.courseName = '';
   })
   .catch(error => console.log(error));
 }
}
```

You may notice that it's quite similar to the previous HTTP call, but this time instead of `.get` we're using `.post`, and passing an object with the key and value of `name`.

After sending the POST request, we then use `this.courses.push(response.data)` to update the client side array as, whilst the server side (our client `db.json` file) is updated, the client state is not.

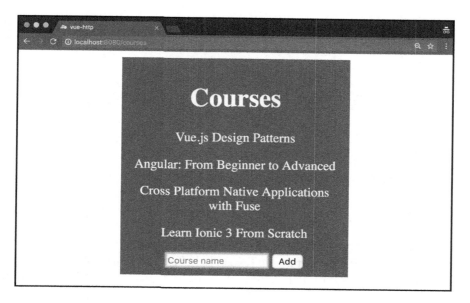

HTTP PUT

The next thing we'd like to be able to do is change items in our list. Perhaps we've made a mistake when submitting the item and we therefore want to edit it. Let's add that functionality.

Firstly, let's tell Vue to keep track of whenever we're editing a course. A user's intention to edit will be whenever they click a course name; we can then add the editing Boolean to our `data` object:

```
data() {
  return {
    ROOT_URL: 'http://localhost:3000/courses/',
    courses: [],
    courseName: '',
    editing: false,
  };
},
```

Our template can then be changed to reflect this:

```
<template>
 <div class="course-list">
  <h1>Courses</h1>
  <div v-for="course in courses" v-bind:key="course.id">
   <p @click="setEdit(course)" v-if="!editing">
   {{course.name}}
   </p>
   <div v-else>
    <input type="text" v-model="course.name">
    <button @click="saveCourse(course)">Save</button>
   </div>
  </div>
  <div v-if="!editing">
   <input type="text" v-model="courseName" placeholder="Course name">
   <button @click="addCourse(courseName)">Add</button>
  </div>
 </div>
</template>
```

What exactly is happening here? Well, we've changed our `courseName` to instead only display when we're not editing (that is, we haven't clicked the name of the course). Instead, using the `v-else` directive, we're displaying an input box and `button` that allows us to save the new `CourseName`.

We're also hiding the add course button at this point to keep things simple.

Here's what the code looks like:

```
setEdit(course) {
 this.editing = !this.editing;
},
saveCourse(course) {
 this.setEdit();
 axios
 .put(`${this.ROOT_URL}/${course.id}`, { ...course })
 .then(response => {
 console.log(response.data);
 })
 .catch(error => console.log(error));
}
```

Here we're using the `.put` method on our `axios` instance pointed at the endpoint of our selected course. As a data parameter we're using the spread operator with `{ ...course }` to destructure the course variable to work with our API.

After this, we merely log the results to the console. Here's what it looks like when we edit the "Vue.js Design Patterns" string to simply say `Vue.js`:

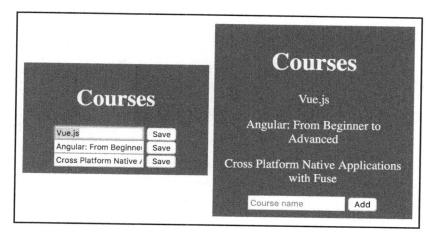

Yay! The last thing we'll be looking at is DELETE and removing items from our database.

HTTP DELETE

To delete items from our list, let's add a `button` so that, when the user enters edit mode (by clicking an item), they can remove that specific course:

```
<div v-else>
  <input type="text" v-model="course.name">
  <button @click="saveCourse(course)">Save</button>
  <button @click="removeCourse(course)">Remove</button>
</div>
```

Our `removeCourse` function then looks as follows:

```
removeCourse(course) {
  axios
    .delete(`${this.ROOT_URL}/${course.id}`)
    .then(response => {
      this.setEdit();
      this.courses = this.courses.filter(c => c.id != course.id);
    })
    .catch(error => console.error(error));
},
```

We're calling the `axios.delete` method and then filtering our `courses` list for every course but the one we've deleted. This then updates our client state and makes it consistent with the database.

In this section of the chapter, we've created ourselves a simple "courses I want to study" list based on our REST API. It could have certainly been abstracted to multiple components, but as this wasn't the core focus of the application we've simply did it all in one.

Coming up next, let's make a real-time chat application with Node and `Socket.io`.

Real-time chat application with Node and Socket.io

In this section, we'll be creating a real-time chat application using Node and `Socket.io`. We'll be writing a small amount of code with Node.js and the Express framework, but it's all the same JavaScript that you know and love.

Run the following in your Terminal to create a new project:

```
# Create a new Vue project
$ vue init webpack-simple vue-chat

# Navigate to directory
$ cd vue-chat

# Install dependencies
$ npm install

# Run application
$ npm run dev
```

We can then create a server folder and initialize a `package.json` for server-specific dependencies like so:

```
# Create a new folder named server
$ mkdir server

# Navigate to directory
$ cd server

# Make a server.js file
$ touch server.js

# Initialise a new package.json
$ npm init -y

# Install dependencies
$ npm install socket.io express --save
```

What is Socket.io?

In our previous example, if we wanted to get new data from the server we'd need to make another HTTP request, whereas with WebSockets we can simply have a consistent event-listener that reacts whenever the event is fired.

To take advantage of this in our chat application, we'll be using `Socket.io`. This is a client and server-side library that allows us to work with WebSockets quickly and easily. It allows us to define and submit events that we can listen to and subsequently perform actions.

Server setup

We can then create a new HTTP server using Express and listen for application connections with `Socket.io` by adding the following to `server.js`:

```
const app = require('express')();
const http = require('http').Server(app);
const io = require('socket.io')(http);
const PORT = 3000;

http.listen(PORT, () => console.log(`Listening on port: ${PORT}`));

io.on('connection', socket => {
  console.log('A user connected.');
});
```

If we then run `node server.js` from within our Terminal inside the `server` folder, we should see the message **Listening on port: 3000**. This means that once we implement `Socket.io` inside of our client application we'll be able to monitor whenever somebody connects to the application.

Client connections

To capture a client connection, we need to install the `Socket.io` into our Vue application. We'll also be using another dependency named `vue-socket.io`, which provides us with a smoother implementation within our Vue applications.

Run the following in your Terminal, ensuring you're in the root directory (that is, not in the `server` folder):

```
# Install socket.io-client and vue-socket.io
$ npm install socket.io-client vue-socket.io --save
```

Setting up Vue and Socket.io

Let's head on over to our `main.js` file so we can register `Socket.io` and the `Vue-Socket.io` plugin. You may remember how to do this from previous chapters:

```
import Vue from 'vue';
import App from './App.vue';
import SocketIo from 'socket.io-client';
import VueSocketIo from 'vue-socket.io';

export const Socket = SocketIo(`http://localhost:3000`);

Vue.use(VueSocketIo, Socket);

new Vue({
  el: '#app',
  render: h => h(App),
});
```

In the preceding code block, we're importing the necessary dependencies and creating a reference to our Socket.io server, which is currently running on port 3000. We're then adding the Vue plugin by using `Vue.use`.

If we've done everything correctly, our client and server should be talking to each other. We should get the following inside of our Terminal:

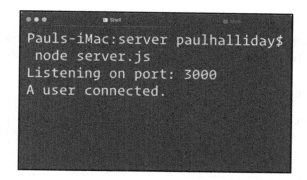

Determining connection status

Now that we've added the Vue-Socket.io plugin, we have access to a sockets object inside of our Vue instance. This allows us to listen to particular events as well as determine whether the user is connected or disconnected from the WebSocket.

Inside of App.vue, let's display a message on screen if we're connected/disconnected from the server:

```
<template>
  <div>
    <h1 v-if="isConnected">Connected to the server.</h1>
    <h1 v-else>Disconnected from the server.</h1>
  </div>
</template>

<script>
export default {
  data() {
    return {
      isConnected: false,
    };
  },
  sockets: {
    connect() {
      this.isConnected = true;
    },
    disconnect() {
      this.isConnected = false;
```

```
      },
    },
  };
</script>
```

There shouldn't be much new here other than the sockets object. Whenever we're connected to the socket, we can run any code we want inside of the `connect()` hook, and the same goes for `disconnect()`. We're simply flipping a Boolean to display a different message on screen with the `v-if` and `v-else` directive(s).

Initially, we get **Connected to the server** as our server is running. If we stop the server with *CTRL* + *C* in our Terminal window, our heading will change to reflect the fact that we no longer have a WebSocket connection. Here's the result:

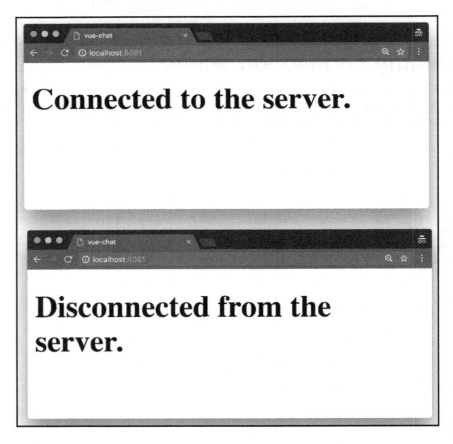

Creating a connection status bar

Let's have some fun with this concept. We can make a components folder and subsequently a new component named `ConnectionStatus.vue`. Inside of this file we can create a status bar that is shown to the user whenever they're online or offline:

```
<template>
  <div>
    <span v-if="isConnected === true" class="bar connected">
      Connected to the server.
    </span>
    <span v-else class="bar disconnected">
      Disconnected from the server.
    </span>
  </div>
</template>

<script>
export default {
  props: ['isConnected'],
};
</script>

<style>
.bar {
  position: absolute;
  bottom: 0;
  left: 0;
  right: 0;
  text-align: center;
  padding: 5px;
}

.connected {
  background: greenyellow;
  color: black;
}

.disconnected {
  background: red;
  color: white;
}
</style>
```

Whilst we only have one screen inside of our current application, we may want to use this component across multiple components, so we can register it globally inside of `main.js`:

```
import App from './App.vue';
import ConnectionStatus from './components/ConnectionStatus.vue';

Vue.component('connection-status', ConnectionStatus);
```

We can then edit our `App.vue` template to use this component and pass the current connection state as a prop:

```
<template>
  <div>
    <connection-status :isConnected="isConnected" />
  </div>
</template>
```

Here's our result:

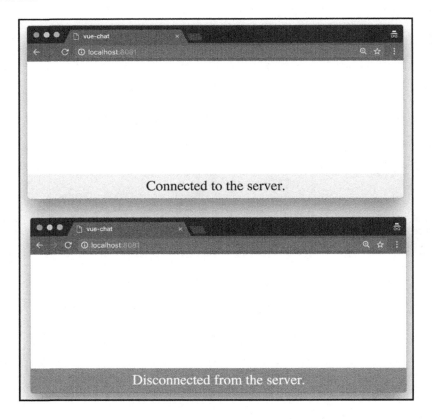

Next, we can make a navigation bar component to make our UI more complete.

Navigation bar

The navigation bar component won't have many uses other than to simply display the name of our application. You could change this to include other functionality such as log in/out, adding new chat channels, or any other chat-specific user actions.

Let's make a new component named `Navbar.vue` in the `components` folder:

```
<template>
  <div v-once>
    <nav class="navbar">
      <span>Socket Chat</span>
    </nav>
  </div>
</template>

<script>
export default {};
</script>

<style>
.navbar {
  background-color: blueviolet;
  padding: 10px;
  margin: 0px;
  text-align: center;
  color: white;
}
</style>
```

You may notice that the `v-once` directive was added on this `div`. This is the first time we've looked at it, but as this component is entirely static we can tell Vue to not listen for any changes and only render it once.

We then have to remove any default padding or margin inside of the HTML body. Create a file named `styles.css` inside of the root directory that contains these attributes:

```
body {
  margin: 0px;
  padding: 0px;
}
```

We can then add this to our `index.html` file like so:

```
<head>
 <meta charset="utf-8">
 <title>vue-chat</title>
 <link rel="stylesheet" href="styles.css">
</head>
```

Next, we'll need to register this component globally. Try and do this by yourself inside `main.js` if you feel you can.

This requires us to import `Navbar` and register it like so:

```
import Navbar from './components/Navbar.vue'

Vue.component('navigation-bar', Navbar);
```

We can then add this to our `App.vue` file:

```
<template>
  <div>
    <navigation-bar />
    <connection-status :isConnected="isConnected" />
  </div>
</template>
```

Next up, let's create our `MessageList` component to hold a list of messages.

Message list

We can display a list of messages on screen by creating a new component with a prop that accepts an array of messages. Create a new component inside the components folder named `MessageList.vue`:

```
<template>
 <div>
  <span v-for="message in messages" :key="message.id">
  <strong>{{message.username}}: </strong> {{message.message}}
  </span>
 </div>
</template>

<script>
export default {
 props: ['messages'],
```

```
};
</script>

<style scoped>
div {
 overflow: scroll;
 height: 150px;
 margin: 10px auto 10px auto;
 padding: 5px;
 border: 1px solid gray;
}
span {
 display: block;
 padding: 2px;
}
</style>
```

This component is fairly simple; all it does is iterate over our messages array using the v-for directive. We pass the messages array into this component using the appropriate prop.

Instead of registering this component globally, let's register it specifically inside of our App.vue component. Whilst we're here, we can also add some dummy data to the messages array:

```
import MessageList from './components/MessageList.vue';

export default {
 data() {
  return {
   isConnected: false,
   messages: [
    {
     id: 1,
     username: 'Paul',
     message: 'Hey!',
    },
    {
     id: 2,
     username: 'Evan',
     message: 'How are you?',
    },
   ],
  };
 },
 components: {
 MessageList,
 },
```

We can then add the `message-list` component to our template:

```
<div class="container">
 <message-list :messages="messages" />
</div>
```

We're passing the messages in as a prop based on the messages array found inside of our data object. We can also add the following styles:

```
<style>
.container {
 width: 300px;
 margin: 0 auto;
}
</style>
```

Doing so will center our message box on the screen and constrain the `width` for demonstration purposes.

We're making progress! Here's our message box:

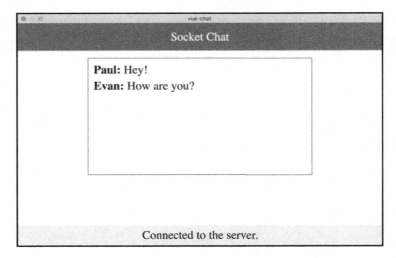

What next? Well, we still need the ability to add messages to our list. Let's work on that next.

Adding messages to the list

Create a new component inside of the components folder named `MessageForm.vue`. This will serve to input messages into the list.

We can start off with the following:

```
<template>
  <form @submit.prevent="sendMessage">
    <div>
      <label for="username">Username:</label>
      <input type="text" name="username" v-model="username">
    </div>
    <div>
      <label for="message">Message:</label>
      <textarea name="message" v-model="message"></textarea>
    </div>
    <button type="submit">Send</button>
  </form>
</template>

<script>
export default {
  data() {
    return {
      username: '',
      message: '',
    };
  },
};
</script>

<style>
input,
textarea {
  margin: 5px;
  width: 100%;
}
</style>
```

This essentially allows us to capture user input for both the selected `username` and `message`. We can then use this information to send data to our `Socket.io` server within the `sendMessage` function.

By adding `@submit.prevent` to our form rather than `@submit`, we're ensuring that we override the default behavior of the submitted form; this is necessary or else our page would otherwise reload.

Let's go and register our form inside of `App.vue`, even though we haven't hooked up any actions yet:

```
import MessageList from './components/MessageList.vue';

export default {
  // Omitted
  components: {
    MessageList,
    MessageForm,
  },
}
```

We can then add this to our template:

```
<template>
  <div>
    <navigation-bar />
    <div class="container">
      <message-list :messages="messages" />
      <message-form />
    </div>
    <connection-status :isConnected="isConnected" />
  </div>
</template>
```

Here's what our application looks like now:

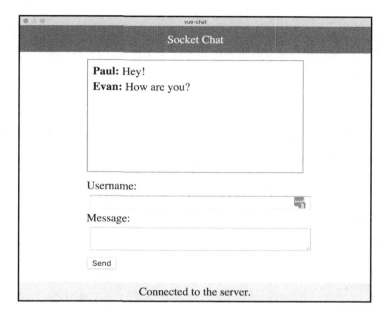

Server-side events with Socket.io

In order to send a new message, we can listen for an event named `chatMessage` within our `server.js` file.

This can be done inside of our original connection event, ensuring that we listen for events on a socket-by-socket basis:

```
io.on('connection', socket => {
  console.log('A user connected.');

  socket.on('chatMessage', message => {
    console.log(message);
  })
});
```

If we then send the `chatMessage` event from our client, it should subsequently log out this message inside of our Terminal. Let's try it out!

Because we've made a change to our `server.js` file, we'll need to restart the Node instance. Hit *CTRL + C* within the Terminal window that is running `server.js` and run node `server.js` again.

Nodemon

Alternatively, you may want to use a module called `nodemon` to automatically do this whenever any changes are made.

Run the following inside of your Terminal:

```
# Install nodemon globally
$ npm install nodemon -g
```

We can then run:

```
# Listen for any changes to our server.js file and restart the server
$ nodemon server.js
```

Great! Let's go back to our `MessageForm` component and create the `sendMessage` function:

```
methods: {
  sendMessage() {
    this.socket.emit('chatMessage', {
      username: this.username,
      message: this.message,
    });
  },
},
```

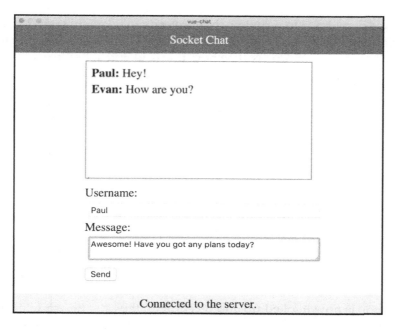

At this point hitting Send doesn't add the message to an array yet, but it does give us the sent message inside of our Terminal! Let's take a look:

```
[nodemon] 1.12.1
[nodemon] to restart at any time, ent
er `rs`
[nodemon] watching: *.*
[nodemon] starting `node server.js`
Listening on port: 3000
A user connected.
{ username: 'Paul',
  message: 'Awesome! Have you got any
 plans today?' }
```

As it turns out, we don't have to write much more code to take advantage of our WebSockets. Let's head back over to the App.vue component and add a function to our sockets object called chatMessage. Notice how this is identical to the event name, meaning that every time this event is fired we can run a particular method:

```
export default {
// Omitted
 sockets: {
  connect() {
   this.isConnected = true;
  },
  disconnect() {
   this.isConnected = false;
  },
  chatMessage(messages) {
   this.messages = messages;
  },
 },
}
```

Our client-side code is now hooked up and listening to the chatMessage event. The problem is that our server-side code isn't currently sending anything to the client! Let's fix this by emitting an event from within the socket:

```
const app = require('express')();
const http = require('http').Server(app);
const io = require('socket.io')(http);
const PORT = 3000;

http.listen(PORT, () => console.log(`Listening on port: ${PORT}`));

const messages = [];

const emitMessages = () => io.emit('chatMessage', messages);

io.on('connection', socket => {
  console.log('A user connected.');

  emitMessages(messages);

  socket.on('chatMessage', message => {
    messages.push(message);

    emitMessages(messages);
  });
});
```

We're keeping the messages in memory with an array named messages. We're also then emitting those messages downstream whenever a client connects to our application (all the previous messages will be shown). As well as this, any time there is a new message added to the array, we're also sending this to all of the clients too.

If we open up two Chrome tabs we should then be able to have a self-directed conversation!

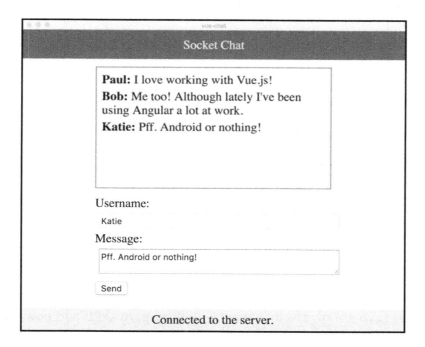

We can then talk to ourselves in the other tab!

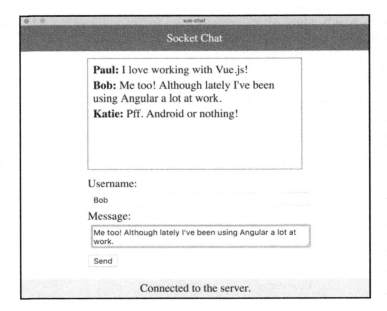

Summary

In this chapter, we learned how to create HTTP requests with Vue using the `Axios` library and `json-server`. This allows us to interact with third-party APIs and power up our Vue applications.

We also looked at how to create a larger application using WebSockets and `Socket.io`. This allows us to have real-time communication with other clients that are connected to our application, allowing for even more possibilities.

We've come a long way! In order to truly take advantage of Vue, we'll need to master the router and look at advanced state management concepts. That is all coming up in the next chapter(s)!

8
Vue Router Patterns

Routing is a vitally important part of any **Single Page Application (SPA)**. This chapter focuses on maximizing the Vue router and looks at everything from routing a user between pages, to parameters, to optimal configuration.

By the end of this chapter, we will have covered the following:

- Implementing routing in a Vue.js application
- Using dynamic route matching to create route parameters
- Passing route parameters as component props

Single Page Applications

Modern JavaScript applications implement a pattern known as an SPA. In its most simplistic form, it can be thought of as an application that displays components based on a URL. As the templates are mapped to routes, there is no need for a page reload, as they can be injected depending on where the user navigated.

This is the job of the router.

By creating our application this way, we're able to increase both perceived and actual speed, because our application is much more dynamic. If we add in the concepts that we learned in the previous chapter (HTTP), you'll find that they go hand in hand with the SPA model.

Using the router

Let's spin up a playground project and install the `vue-router` library. This allows us to take advantage of routing inside our application and give us the power of a modern SPA.

Run the following commands in your Terminal:

```
# Create a new Vue project
$ vue init webpack-simple vue-router-basics

# Navigate to directory
$ cd vue-router-basics

# Install dependencies
$ npm install

# Install Vue Router
$ npm install vue-router

# Run application
$ npm run dev
```

As we're using webpack as part of our build system, we've installed the router with npm. We can then initialize the router inside of `src/main.js`:

```
import Vue from 'vue';
import VueRouter from 'vue-router';

import App from './App.vue';

Vue.use(VueRouter);

new Vue({
  el: '#app',
  render: h => h(App)
});
```

This effectively registers `VueRouter` as a global plugin. A plugin simply is just a function that receives `Vue` and `options` as parameters and allows libraries such as `VueRouter` to add functionality to our Vue application.

Creating routes

We can then define two small components inside our `main.js` file that simply have a template that shows `h1` with some text inside:

```
const Hello = { template: `<h1>Hello</h1>` };
const World = { template: `<h1>World</h1>` };
```

Then, in order to display these components on screen at particular URLs (such as `/hello` and `/world`), we can define routes inside our application:

```
const routes = [
  { path: '/hello', component: Hello },
  { path: '/world', component: World }
];
```

Now that we've defined what components we want to use as well as the routes inside of our application, we'll need to create a new instance of `VueRouter` and pass along the routes.

Although we've used `Vue.use(VueRouter)`, we still need to create a new instance of `VueRouter` and initialize our routes. This is because merely registering `VueRouter` as a plugin gives us access to the router option within our Vue instance(s):

```
const router = new VueRouter({
  routes
});
```

We then need to pass the `router` to our root Vue instance:

```
new Vue({
  el: '#app',
  router,
  render: h => h(App)
});
```

Finally, to display our routed components inside of our `App.vue` component, we need to add the `router-view` component inside the `template`:

```
<template>
  <div id="app">
    <router-view/>
  </div>
</template>
```

If we then navigate to /#/hello/ or /#/world, the appropriate component is displayed:

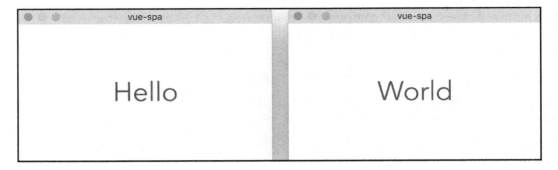

Dynamic routes

We can also dynamically match routes depending on a particular parameter. This is done by specifying a route with a colon before the parameter name. Here's an example using a similar greeting component:

```
// Components
const Hello = { template: `<h1>Hello</h1>` };
const HelloName = { template: `<h1>Hello {{ $route.params.name}}` }

// Routes
const routes = [
 { path: '/hello', component: Hello },
 { path: '/hello/:name', component: HelloName },
]
```

If our user navigates to /hello, they'll see h1 with the text Hello. Otherwise, if they navigate to /hello/{name} (that is, Paul), they'll see h1 with the text Hello Paul.

We've made a lot of progress, but it's important to know that when we navigate to parameterized URLs, component lifecycle hooks aren't fired again if the parameter changes (that is, from /hello/paul to /hello/katie). We'll look at this soon!

Route props

Let's change our /hello/name route to pass the name parameter as a component prop, which can be done by adding the props: true flag to the route:

```
const routes = [
  { path: '/hello', component: Hello },
  { path: '/hello/:name', component: HelloName, props: true},
]
```

We can then update our component to take in a prop with an id of name and also log this to the console within the life cycle hook:

```
const HelloName = {
  props: ['name'],
  template: `<h1>Hello {{ name }}</h1>`,
  created() {
    console.log(`Hello ${this.name}`)
  }
}
```

If we then try and navigate to different dynamic routes, we'll see that the created hook only fires once (unless we refresh the page) even though our page shows the correct name:

Component Navigation Guards

How do we fix the lifecycle hook problem? In this instance, we can use what's known as a Navigation Guard. This allows us to hook into different lifecycles of the router, such as the beforeRouteEnter, beforeRouteUpdate, and beforeRouteLeave methods.

beforeRouteUpdate

Let's use the beforeRouteUpdate method to access information about the route change:

```
const HelloName = {
  props: ['name'],
  template: `<h1>Hello {{ name }}</h1>`,
  beforeRouteUpdate(to, from, next) {
    console.log(to);
    console.log(from);
    console.log(`Hello ${to.params.name}`)
  },
}
```

If we check the JavaScript console after navigating to a different route under /hello/{name}, we'll be able to see which route the user is going to and where they are coming from. The to and from objects also give us access to params, queries, the full path, and much more.

While we correctly get the log statements, if we try and navigate between routes, you'll note that our application doesn't update with the parameter name prop. This is because we haven't used the next function after we've finished doing any computations within the guard. Let's add that in:

```
beforeRouteUpdate(to, from, next) {
  console.log(to);
  console.log(from);
  console.log(`Hello ${to.params.name}`)
  next();
},
```

beforeRouteEnter

We can also take advantage of `beforeRouteEnter` to perform actions prior to entering the component route. Here's an example:

```
beforeRouteEnter(to, from, next) {
  console.log(`I'm called before entering the route!`)
  next();
}
```

We still have to call `next` to pass the stack down to the next route handler.

beforeRouteLeave

We can also hook into `beforeRouteLeave` to perform actions whenever we're navigating away from a route. As we're already on this route within the context of this hook, we have access to the component instance. Let's look at an example:

```
beforeRouteLeave(to, from, next) {
console.log(`I'm called before leaving the route!`)
console.log(`I have access to the component instance, here's proof!
Name: ${this.name}`);
next();
}
```

Once again, we have to call `next` in this instance.

Global router hooks

We've looked at component Navigation Guards and while these work on a component-by-component basis, you may want to establish global hooks that listen to navigation events.

beforeEach

We can use `router.beforeEach` to listen for routing events globally across the application. This is worth using if you have authentication checks or other pieces of functionality that should be used in every route.

Here's an example that simply logs out the route the user is going to and coming from. Each one of the following examples assume that the router exists in scope similar to the following:

```
const router = new VueRouter({
  routes
})

router.beforeEach((to, from, next) => {
 console.log(`Route to`, to)
 console.log(`Route from`, from)
 next();
});
```

Once again, we have to call `next()` to trigger the next route guard.

beforeResolve

The `beforeResolve` global route guard is triggered just before navigation is confirmed, but it's important to know that this is only after all component-specific guards and async components have been resolved.

Here's an example:

```
router.beforeResolve((to, from, next) => {
 console.log(`Before resolve:`)
 console.log(`Route to`, to)
 console.log(`Route from`, from)
 next();
});
```

afterEach

We can also hook into the global `afterEach` function that allows us to perform the action(s), but we can't affect navigation and thus only have access to the `to` and `from` parameters:

```
router.afterEach((to, from) => {
 console.log(`After each:`)
 console.log(`Route to`, to)
 console.log(`Route from`, from)
});
```

Resolution stack

Now that we've familiarized ourselves with the various different route lifecycle hooks on offer, it's worth investigating the entire resolution stack whenever we attempt to navigate to another route:

1. **Trigger a route change**:
   This is the first stage of any route lifecycle and is triggered any time we *attempt* to navigate to a new route. An example would be going from /hello/Paul to /hello/Katie. No Navigation Guards have been triggered at this point.

2. **Trigger component leave guards**:
   Next, any leave guards are triggered, such as beforeRouteLeave, on loaded components.

3. **Trigger global beforeEach guards**:
   As global route middleware can be created with beforeEach, these functions will be called prior to any route update.

4. **Trigger local beforeRouteUpdate guards in reused components**:
   As we saw earlier, whenever we navigate to the same route with a different parameter, the lifecycle hooks aren't fired twice. Instead, we use beforeRouteUpdate to trigger lifecycle changes.

5. **Trigger beforeRouteEnter in components**:
   This is called each time prior to navigating to any route. At this stage, the component isn't rendered, so it doesn't have access to the this component instance.

6. **Resolve asynchronous route components**:
   It then attempts to resolve any asynchronous components in your project. Here's an example of one:

   ```
   const MyAsyncComponent = () => ({
   component: import ('./LazyComponent.vue'),
   loading: LoadingComponent,
   error: ErrorComponent,
   delay: 150,
   timeout: 3000
   })
   ```

7. **Trigger beforeRouteEnter in successfully activated components**:
   We now have access to the beforeRouteEnter hook and can perform any action(s) prior to resolving the route.

8. **Trigger global beforeResolve hooks**:
   Providing in-component guards and async route components have been resolved, we can now hook into the global `router.beforeResolve` method that allows us to perform action(s) at this stage.

9. **Navigation**:
   All prior Navigation Guards have been fired, and the user is now successfully navigated to a route.

10. **Trigger afterEach hooks**:
    Although the user has been navigated to the route, it doesn't stop there. Next, the router triggers a global `afterEach` hook that has access to the `to` and `from` parameters. As the route has already been resolved at this stage, it doesn't have the next parameter and thus cannot affect navigation.

11. **Trigger DOM updates**:
    Routes have been resolved, and Vue can appropriately trigger DOM updates.

12. **Trigger callbacks within next in beforeRouteEnter**:
    As `beforeRouteEnter` does not have access to the component's `this` context, the `next` parameter takes a callback that resolves to the component instance on navigation. An example can be seen here:

```
beforeRouteEnter (to, from, next) {
  next(comp => {
    // 'comp' inside this closure is equal to the component instance
  })
```

Programmatic navigation

We're not limited to template navigation using `router-link`; we can also programmatically navigate the user to different routes from within our JavaScript. Inside of our `App.vue`, let's expose the `<router-view>` and give the user the ability to select a button that will navigate them to either the `/hello` or `/hello/:name` route:

```
<template>
  <div id="app">
    <nav>
      <button @click="navigateToRoute('/hello')">/Hello</button>
      <button
      @click="navigateToRoute('/hello/Paul')">/Hello/Name</button>
    </nav>
    <router-view></router-view>
  </div>
</template>
```

We can then add a method that pushes a new route onto the route stack:

```
<script>
export default {
  methods: {
    navigateToRoute(routeName) {
      this.$router.push({ path: routeName });
    },
  },
};
</script>
```

At this point, any time we select a button, it should subsequently navigate the user to the appropriate route. The `$router.push()` function can take a variety of different arguments, depending on how you have your routes set up. Here are some examples:

```
// Navigate with string literal
this.$router.push('hello')

// Navigate with object options
this.$router.push({ path: 'hello' })

// Add parameters
this.$router.push({ name: 'hello', params: { name: 'Paul' }})

// Using query parameters /hello?name=paul
this.$router.push({ path: 'hello', query: { name: 'Paul' }})
```

router.replace

Instead of pushing a navigation item on the stack, we can also replace the current history stack with `router.replace`. Here's an example of this:

```
this.$router.replace({ path: routeName });
```

router.go

If we want to navigate the user backward or forward, we can use `router.go`; this is essentially an abstraction over the `window.history` API. Let's take a look at some examples:

```
// Navigate forward one record
this.$router.go(1);
```

```
// Navigate backward one record
this.$router.go(-1);

// Navigate forward three records
this.$router.go(3);

// Navigate backward three records
this.$router.go(-3);
```

Lazy loading routes

We can also lazy load our routes to take advantage of code splitting with webpack. This allows us to have greater performance than when eagerly loading our routes. To do this, we can create a small playground project. Run the following in your Terminal:

```
# Create a new Vue project
$ vue init webpack-simple vue-lazy-loading

# Navigate to directory
$ cd vue-lazy-loading

# Install dependencies
$ npm install

# Install Vue Router
$ npm install vue-router

# Run application
$ npm run dev
```

Let's start off by creating two components, named `Hello.vue` and `World.vue`, inside `src/components`:

```
// Hello.vue
<template>
  <div>
    <h1>Hello</h1>
    <router-link to="/world">Next</router-link>
  </div>
</template>

<script>
export default {};
</script>
```

Now we have created our `Hello.vue` component, let's create the second `World.vue` like so:

```
// World.vue
<template>
  <div>
    <h1>World</h1>
    <router-link to="/hello">Back</router-link>
  </div>
</template>

<script>
export default {};
</script>
```

We can then initialize our router as we usually do, inside `main.js`:

```
import Vue from 'vue';
import VueRouter from 'vue-router';

Vue.use(VueRouter);
```

The main difference has to do with the way in which to import our components. This requires the use of the `syntax-dynamic-import` Babel plugin. Install it into your project by running the following in your Terminal:

```
$ npm install --save-dev babel-plugin-syntax-dynamic-import
```

We can then update `.babelrc` to use the new plugin:

```
{
  "presets": [["env", { "modules": false }], "stage-3"],
  "plugins": ["syntax-dynamic-import"]
}
```

Finally, this allows us to import our components asynchronously, like this:

```
const Hello = () => import('./components/Hello');
const World = () => import('./components/World');
```

We can then define our routes and initialize the router, this time referencing the asynchronous import:

```
const routes = [
  { path: '/', redirect: '/hello' },
  { path: '/hello', component: Hello },
  { path: '/World', component: World },
```

```
];

const router = new VueRouter({
  routes,
});

new Vue({
  el: '#app',
  router,
  render: h => h(App),
});
```

We can then see its results by looking in Chrome via **Developer Tools | Network tab** while navigating through our application:

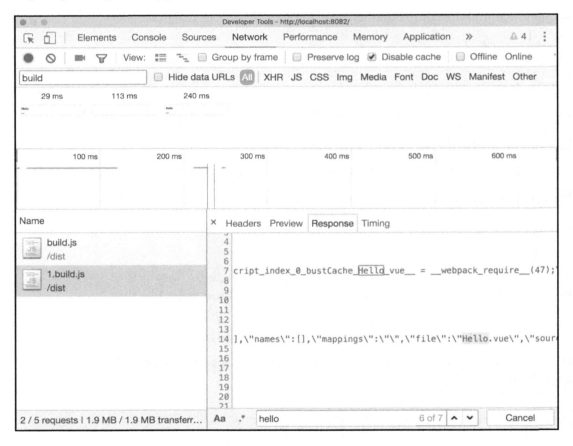

Each route is added to its own bundle file and subsequently gives us improved
performance as the initial bundle is much smaller:

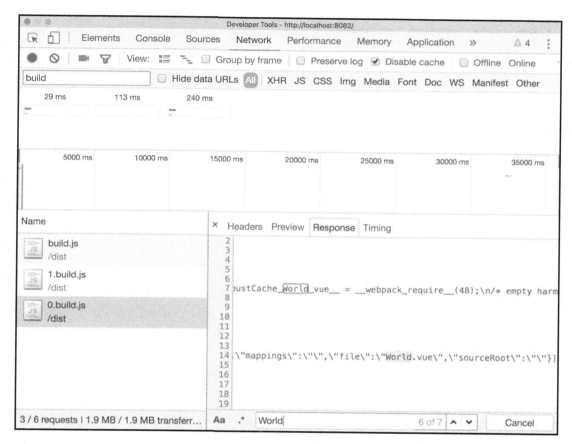

An SPA project

Let's create a project that uses a RESTful API and the routing concepts that we've just
learned. Create a new project by running the following in your Terminal:

```
# Create a new Vue project
$ vue init webpack-simple vue-spa

# Navigate to directory
$ cd vue-spa
```

```
# Install dependencies
$ npm install

# Install Vue Router and Axios
$ npm install vue-router axios

# Run application
$ npm run dev
```

Enabling the router

We can start off by enabling the VueRouter plugin within our application. To do this, we can create a new file inside src/router named index.js. We'll use this file to contain all the router-specific configuration, but we'll separate out each route into different files depending on the underlying feature.

Let's import and add the router plugin:

```
import Vue from 'vue';
import VueRouter from 'vue-router';

Vue.use(VueRouter)
```

Defining routes

To separate out the routes into different files within our application, we can firstly create a file under src/components/user named user.routes.js. Each time we have a different feature set (that requires routes), we can create our own *.routes.js file that can be imported into the router's index.js.

For now, we can just export a new empty array:

```
export const userRoutes = [];
```

We can then add the routes to our index.js (even though we have none defined yet):

```
import { userRoutes } from '../components/user/user.routes';

const routes = [...userRoutes];
```

We're using the ES2015+ spread operator, which allows us to use each object in the array instead of the array itself.

To then initialize the router, we can then create a new `VueRouter` and pass along the routes, as follows:

```
const router = new VueRouter({
  // This is ES2015+ shorthand for routes: routes
  routes,
});
```

Finally, let's export the router so that it can be used inside our main Vue instance:

```
export default router;
```

Inside `main.js`, let's import the router and add it to the instance, as shown:

```
import Vue from 'vue';
import App from './App.vue';
import router from './router';

new Vue({
  el: '#app',
  router,
  render: h => h(App),
});
```

Creating the UserList route

The first section of our application will be a home page that displays a list of users from an API. We've used this example in the past, so you should be familiar with the steps involved. Let's create a new component under `src/components/user` named `UserList.vue`.

The component will look something like this:

```
<template>
  <ul>
    <li v-for="user in users" :key="user.id">
      {{user.name}}
    </li>
  </ul>
</template>

<script>
export default {
  data() {
    return {
      users: [
        {
```

```
        id: 1,
        name: 'Leanne Graham',
      }
    ],
  };
},
};
</script>
```

Feel free to add your own test data at this point. We'll be requesting this data from the API momentarily.

As we've created our component, we can then add a route to `user.routes.js`, which displays this component whenever the `'/'` (or a path of your choice) is activated:

```
import UserList from './UserList';

export const userRoutes = [{ path: '/', component: UserList }];
```

In order to show this route, we need to update `App.vue` to subsequently inject the content into a `router-view` node. Let's update `App.vue` to handle this:

```
<template>
 <div>
  <router-view></router-view>
 </div>
</template>

<script>
export default {};
</script>

<style>

</style>
```

Our application should then display a single user. Let's create an HTTP utility to get data from an API.

Getting data from an API

Create a new file under `src/utils` named `api.js`. This will be used to create a base instance of `Axios`, which we can then perform HTTP requests on:

```js
import axios from 'axios';

export const API = axios.create({
  baseURL: `https://jsonplaceholder.typicode.com/`
})
```

We can then use the `beforeRouteEnter` Navigation Guard to get user data whenever someone navigates to the ' / ' route:

```html
<template>
  <ul>
    <li v-for="user in users" :key="user.id">
      {{user.name}}
    </li>
  </ul>
</template>

<script>
import { API } from '../../utils/api';
export default {
  data() {
    return {
      users: [],
    };
  },
  beforeRouteEnter(to, from, next) {
    API.get(`users`)
      .then(response => next(vm => (vm.users = response.data)))
      .catch(error => next(error));
  },
};
</script>
```

We then find that we get a list of users on screen, as illustrated in the following screenshot, each represented as a different list item. The next step is to create a `detail` component, register the detail route, and find a way to link to that route:

Creating a detail page

In order to create a detail page, we can create `UserDetail.vue` and follow steps similar to the previous component:

```
<template>
  <div class="container">
    <div class="user">
      <div class="user__name">
        <h1>{{userInfo.name}}</h1>
        <p>Person ID {{$route.params.userId}}</p>
        <p>Username: {{userInfo.username}}</p>
        <p>Email: {{userInfo.email}}</p>
      </div>
      <div class="user__address" v-if="userInfo && userInfo.address">
        <h1>Address</h1>
        <p>Street: {{userInfo.address.street}}</p>
        <p>Suite: {{userInfo.address.suite}}</p>
        <p>City: {{userInfo.address.city}}</p>
        <p>Zipcode: {{userInfo.address.zipcode}}</p>
```

```
        <p>Lat: {{userInfo.address.geo.lat}} Lng:
        {{userInfo.address.geo.lng}} </p>
      </div>

      <div class="user__other" >
        <h1>Other</h1>
        <p>Phone: {{userInfo.phone}}</p>
        <p>Website: {{userInfo.website}}</p>
        <p v-if="userInfo && userInfo.company">Company:
        {{userInfo.company.name}}</p>
      </div>
    </div>
  </div>
</template>

<script>
import { API } from '../../utils/api';

export default {
  data() {
    return {
      userInfo: {},
    };
  },
  beforeRouteEnter(to, from, next) {
    next(vm =>
      API.get(`users/${to.params.userId}`)
        .then(response => (vm.userInfo = response.data))
        .catch(err => console.error(err))
    )
  },
};
</script>

<style>
.container {
 line-height: 2.5em;
 text-align: center;
}
</style>
```

As there should never be more than one user inside of our detail page, the `userInfo` variable has been created as a JavaScript object rather than an array.

We can then add the new component to our `user.routes.js`:

```
import UserList from './UserList';
import UserDetail from './UserDetail';

export const userRoutes = [
  { path: '/', component: UserList },
  { path: '/:userId', component: UserDetail },
];
```

In order to link to this component, we can add `router-link` within our `UserList` component:

```
<template>
  <ul>
    <li v-for="user in users" :key="user.id">
      <router-link :to="{ path: `/${user.id}` }">
      {{user.name}}
      </router-link>
    </li>
  </ul>
</template>
```

If we then take a look in our browser we can see that there is only one user listed with the information underneath coming from the user detail linked to that one user:

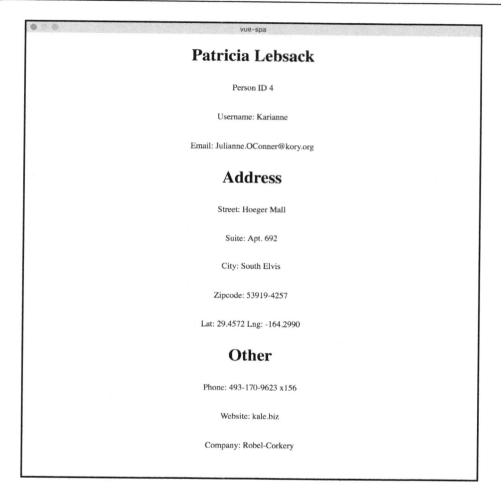

Child routes

We can also access posts from our API, and as a result, we can display both the posts' information alongside our user information. Let's create a new component named `UserPosts.vue`:

```
<template>
  <div>
    <ul>
      <li v-for="post in posts" :key="post.id">{{post.title}}</li>
    </ul>
```

```
    </div>
  </template>

  <script>
  import { API } from '../../utils/api';
  export default {
    data() {
      return {
        posts: [],
      };
    },
    beforeRouteEnter(to, from, next) {
        next(vm =>
            API.get(`posts?userId=${to.params.userId}`)
            .then(response => (vm.posts = response.data))
            .catch(err => console.error(err))
        )
    },
  };
  </script>
```

This allows us to get posts based on our userId route parameter. In order to display this component as a child view, we'll need to register it as such within the user.routes.js:

```
import UserList from './UserList';
import UserDetail from './UserDetail';
import UserPosts from './UserPosts';

export const userRoutes = [
  { path: '/', component: UserList },
  {
    path: '/:userId',
    component: UserDetail,
    children: [{ path: '/:userId', component: UserPosts }],
  },
];
```

We can then add another `<router-view>` tag inside our `UserDetail.vue` component to display the child route. The template now looks like this:

```
<template>
  <div class="container">
    <div class="user">
        // Omitted
    </div>
    <div class="posts">
      <h1>Posts</h1>
      <router-view></router-view>
    </div>
  </div>
</template>
```

To top it off, we've also added some styles that display the user information on the left and posts on the right:

```
<style>
.container {
  line-height: 2.5em;
  text-align: center;
}
.user {
  display: inline-block;
  width: 49%;
}
.posts {
  vertical-align: top;
  display: inline-block;
  width: 49%;
}
ul {
  list-style-type: none;
}
</style>
```

If we then head to our browser, we can see how the data appears just as we had planned, with the user information displaying on the left and the posts on the right:

Ta-da! We've now created a Vue application with multiple routes, child routes, parameters, and more!

Summary

In this section, we learned about the Vue Router and how we can use it to create Single Page Applications. As a result, we covered everything from initializing the router plugin to defining routes, components, Navigation Guards, and much more. We now have the necessary knowledge to create Vue applications that scale past a singular component.

Now that we have expanded our knowledge and understand how to use the Vue Router, we can move on to handling state management with Vuex in the next chapter.

9
State Management with Vuex

In this chapter, we'll be looking at State Management Patterns with Vuex. Vuex may not be needed for every application created, but it is extremely important that you have an understanding of what it is when it becomes appropriate to use it, and how to implement it.

By the end of this chapter, you will have done the following:

- Understood what Vuex is and why you should use it
- Created your first Vuex store
- Investigated actions, mutations, getters, and modules
- Used the Vue devtools to step through Vuex mutations as they happen

What is Vuex?

State management is an important part of modern-day web applications, and managing this state as the application grows is a problem every project faces. Vuex looks to help us achieve better state management by enforcing a centralized store, essentially a single source of truth within our application. It follows design principles similar to that of Flux and Redux and also integrates with the official Vue devtools for a great development experience.

So far, I've spoken about *state* and *managing state*, but you may still be confused as to what this really means for your application. Let's define these terms in a little more depth.

State Management Pattern (SMP)

We can define a state as the current value(s) of a variable/object within our component or application. If we think about our functions as simple `INPUT -> OUTPUT` machines, the values stored outside of these functions make up the current condition (state) of our application.

Note how I've made a distinction between **component level** and **application level** state. The component level state can be defined as state confined to one component (that is, the data function within our component). Application level state is similar but is often used across multiple components or services.

As our application continues to grow, passing state across multiple components gets more difficult. We saw earlier in the book that we can use an Event bus (that is, a global Vue instance) to pass data around, and while this works, it's much better to define our state as part of a singular centralized store. This allows us to reason about the data in our application much easier, as we can start defining **actions** and **mutations** that always generate a new version of state, and managing state become much more systemized.

Event bus is a simple approach to state management relying on a singular view instance and may be beneficial in small Vuex projects, but in the majority of cases, Vuex should be used. As our application becomes larger, clearly defining our actions and intended side effects with Vuex allows us to better manage and scale the project.

A great example of how all this fits together can be seen in the following screenshot (https://vuex.vuejs.org/en/intro.html):

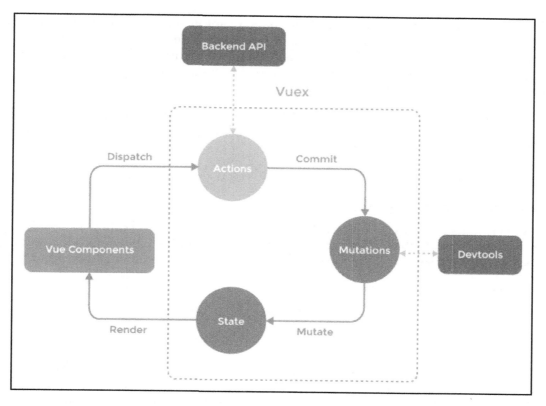

Vuex state flow

Let's break down this example into a step-by-step process:

1. Initial **State** is rendered inside of a Vue component.
2. A Vue component dispatches an **Action** to get some data from a **Backend API**.
3. This then fires a **Commit** event that is handled by a **Mutation**. This **Mutation** returns a new version of the state containing the data from the **Backend API**.
4. The process can then be seen in the Vue **Devtools**, and you have the ability to "time travel" between different versions of the previous state that takes place within the application.
5. The new **State** is then rendered inside of the **Vue Components**.

The main component of our Vuex application(s) is, therefore, the store, our single source of truth across all component(s). The store can be read but not directly altered; it must have mutation functions to carry out any changes. Although this pattern may seem strange at first, if you've never used a state container before, this design allows us to add new features to our application in a consistent manner.

As Vuex is natively designed to work with Vue, the store is reactive by default. This means any changes that happen from within the store can be seen in real time without the need for any hacks.

Thinking about state

As a thought exercise, let's start off by defining the goals for our application as well as any state, actions, and potential mutations. You don't have to add the following code to your application just yet, so feel free to read on, and we'll bring it all together at the end.

Let's start off by considering the state as a collection of key/value pairs:

```
const state = {
 count: 0 // number
}
```

For our counter application, we just need one element of state—the current count. This will likely have a default value of 0 and will be of type number. As this is likely the only state inside of our application, you can consider this state to be application level at this point.

Next, let's think about any action types that the user may want to take our counter application.

These three action types can then be dispatched to the store and thus we can perform the following mutations, returning a new version of state each time:

- **Increment**: Add one to the current count (0 -> 1)
- **Decrement**: Remove one from the current count (1 -> 0)
- **Reset**: Set the current count back to zero (n -> 0)

We can imagine that at this point, our user interface will be updated with the correct bound version of our count. Let's implement this and make it a reality.

Using Vuex

Now that we've had a detailed look at what makes up an application driven by Vuex, let's make a playground project to take advantage of these features!

Run the following in your Terminal:

```
# Create a new Vue project
$ vue init webpack-simple vuex-counter

# Navigate to directory
$ cd vuex-counter

# Install dependencies
$ npm install

# Install Vuex
$ npm install vuex

# Run application
$ npm run dev
```

Creating a new store

Let's start off by creating a file named index.js inside src/store. This is the file we'll use to create our new store and bring together the various components.

We can start by importing both Vue and Vuex as well as telling Vue that we'd like to use the Vuex plugin:

```
import Vue from 'vue';
import Vuex from 'vuex';

Vue.use(Vuex);
```

We can then export a new Vuex.Store with a state object that contains all of our application states. We're exporting this so that we can import the state in other components when necessary:

```
export default new Vuex.Store({
  state: {
    count: 0,
  },
});
```

Defining action types

We can then create a file inside `src/store` named `mutation-types.js`, which contains the various actions that the user may take within our application:

```
export const INCREMENT = 'INCREMENT';
export const DECREMENT = 'DECREMENT';
export const RESET = 'RESET';
```

Although we don't have to explicitly define our actions like this, it's a good idea to use constants where possible. This allows us to take better advantage of tooling and linting techniques, as well as allowing us to infer the actions within our entire application at a glance.

Actions

We can use these action types to commit a new action to be subsequently handled by our mutations. Create a file inside `src/store` named `actions.js`:

```
import * as types from './mutation-types';

export default {
  [types.INCREMENT]({ commit }) {
    commit(types.INCREMENT);
  },
  [types.DECREMENT]({ commit }) {
    commit(types.DECREMENT);
  },
  [types.RESET]({ commit }) {
    commit(types.RESET);
  },
};
```

Inside each method, we're destructuring the returned `store` object to only take the `commit` function. If we didn't do this, we'd have to call the `commit` function like this:

```
export default {
 [types.INCREMENT](store) {
  store.commit(types.INCREMENT);
 }
}
```

If we revisit our state diagram, we can see that after committing an action, the action is picked up by the mutator.

Mutations

A mutation is the only method in which the state of the store can be changed; this is done by committing/dispatching an action, as seen earlier. Let's create a new file inside `src/store` named `mutations.js` and add the following:

```javascript
import * as types from './mutation-types';

export default {
  [types.INCREMENT](state) {
    state.count++;
  },
  [types.DECREMENT](state) {
    state.count--;
  },
  [types.RESET](state) {
    state.count = 0;
  },
};
```

You'll note that once again, we're using our action types to define the method names; this is possible with a new feature from ES2015+ named computed property names. Now, any time that an action is committed/dispatched, the mutator will know how to handle this and return a new state.

Getters

We can now commit actions and have these actions return a new version of the state. The next step is to create getters so that we can return sliced parts of our state across our application. Let's create a new file inside `src/store` named `getters.js` and add the following:

```javascript
export default {
  count(state) {
    return state.count;
  },
};
```

As we have a minuscule example, the use of a getter for this property isn't entirely necessary, but as we scale our application(s), we'll need to use getters to filter state. Think of these as computed properties for values in the state, so if we wanted to return a modified version of this property for the view-layer, we could as follows:

```
export default {
  count(state) {
    return state.count > 3 ? 'Above three!' : state.count;
  },
};
```

Combining elements

In order to pull this all together, we have to revisit our store/index.js file and add the appropriate state, actions, getters, and mutations:

```
import Vue from 'vue';
import Vuex from 'vuex';

import actions from './actions';
import getters from './getters';
import mutations from './mutations';

Vue.use(Vuex);

export default new Vuex.Store({
  state: {
    count: 0,
  },
  actions,
  getters,
  mutations,
});
```

In our App.vue, we can create a template that will give us the current count as well as some buttons to increment, decrement, and reset state:

```
<template>
  <div>
    <h1>{{count}}</h1>
    <button @click="increment">+</button>
    <button @click="decrement">-</button>
    <button @click="reset">R</button>
  </div>
</template>
```

Whenever the user clicks on a button, an action is dispatched from within one of the following methods:

```
import * as types from './store/mutation-types';

export default {
  methods: {
    increment() {
      this.$store.dispatch(types.INCREMENT);
    },
    decrement() {
      this.$store.dispatch(types.DECREMENT);
    },
    reset() {
      this.$store.dispatch(types.RESET);
    },
  },
}
```

Once again, we're using constants to make for a better development experience. Next, in order to take advantage of the getter we created earlier, let's define a computed property:

```
export default {
  // Omitted
  computed: {
    count() {
      return this.$store.getters.count;
    },
  },
}
```

We then have an application that displays the current count and can be incremented, decremented, or reset:

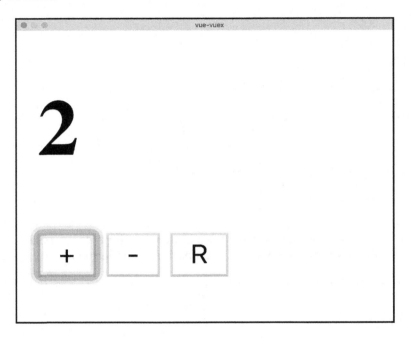

Payloads

What if we wanted to let the user decide how much they wanted to increment the count? Let's say we had a textbox that we could add a number and increment the count by that much. If the textbox was set to 0 or was empty, we'd increment the count by 1.

Our template would, therefore, look like this:

```
<template>
  <div>
    <h1>{{count}}</h1>

    <input type="text" v-model="amount">

    <button @click="increment">+</button>
    <button @click="decrement">-</button>
    <button @click="reset">R</button>
  </div>
</template>
```

We'd place the amount value on our local component state, as this doesn't necessarily need to be part of the main Vuex Store. This is an important realization to make, as it means we can still have local data/computed values if necessary. We can also update our methods to pass the amount through to our actions/mutations:

```
export default {
  data() {
    return {
      amount: 0,
    };
  },
  methods: {
    increment() {
      this.$store.dispatch(types.INCREMENT, this.getAmount);
    },
    decrement() {
      this.$store.dispatch(types.DECREMENT, this.getAmount);
    },
    reset() {
      this.$store.dispatch(types.RESET);
    },
  },
  computed: {
    count() {
      return this.$store.getters.count;
    },
    getAmount() {
      return Number(this.amount) || 1;
    },
  },
};
```

We then have to update `actions.js` as this now receives both the `state` object and our `amount` as an argument. When we use `commit`, let's also pass the `amount` through to the mutation:

```
import * as types from './mutation-types';

export default {
  [types.INCREMENT]({ commit }, amount) {
    commit(types.INCREMENT, amount);
  },
  [types.DECREMENT]({ commit }, amount) {
    commit(types.DECREMENT, amount);
  },
  [types.RESET]({ commit }) {
    commit(types.RESET);
```

```
    },
  };
```

Therefore, our mutations look similar to before, but this time we increment/decrement based on the amount:

```
export default {
  [types.INCREMENT](state, amount) {
    state.count += amount;
  },
  [types.DECREMENT](state, amount) {
    state.count -= amount;
  },
  [types.RESET](state) {
    state.count = 0;
  },
};
```

Ta-da! We can now increment the count based on a text value:

Vuex and Vue devtools

Now that we have a consistent way of interacting with our store via actions, we can take advantage of the Vue devtools to see our state over time. If you haven't installed the Vue devtools already, visit `Chapter 2`, *Proper Creation of Vue Projects*, to find more information regarding this.

We'll be using the counter application as an example, to ensure that you have this project running, and right click on **Inspect Element** from within Chrome (or your browser's equivalent). If we head over to the **Vue** tab and select **Vuex**, we can see that the counter has been loaded with the initial application state:

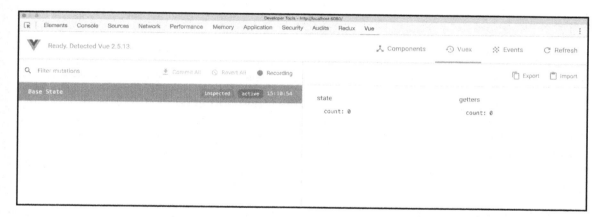

From the preceding screenshot, you can see the count state member as well as the value of any getters. Let's click on the **increment** button a few times and see what happens:

Awesome! We can see the **INCREMENT** action as well as a subsequent change to the **state and getters**, and more information about the **mutation** itself. Let's see how we can time travel throughout our state:

In the preceding screenshot, I've selected the **time travel** button on the first action. You can then see that our state is reverted to **count: 1**, and this is reflected in the rest of the metadata. The application is then updated to reflect this change in state, so we can literally step through each action and see the results on screen. Not only does this help with debugging, but any new state that we add to our application will follow the same process and be visible in this manner.

Let's hit the **commit** button on an action:

As you can see, this merges all of our actions up to when we hit **commit** to then be part of our **Base State**. As a result, the **count** property is then equal to the action you committed to **Base State**.

Modules and scalability

At the moment, we have everything in root state. As our application gets larger, it would be a good idea to take advantage of modules so that we can appropriately split our container into different chunks. Let's turn our counter state into its own module by creating a new folder inside `store` named `modules/count`.

We can then move the `actions.js`, `getters.js`, `mutations.js`, and `mutation-types.js` files into the count module folder. After doing so, we can create an `index.js` file inside the folder that exports the `state`, `actions`, `getters`, and `mutations` for this module only:

```
import actions from './actions';
import getters from './getters';
import mutations from './mutations';

export const countStore = {
  state: {
    count: 0,
  },
  actions,
  getters,
  mutations,
};

export * from './mutation-types';
```

I've also elected to export the mutation types from the `index.js` file, so we can use these within our components on a per-module basis by importing from `store/modules/count` only. As we're importing more than one thing within this file, I gave the store the name of `countStore`. Let's define the new module inside `store/index.js`:

```
import Vue from 'vue';
import Vuex from 'vuex';
import { countStore } from './modules/count';

Vue.use(Vuex);

export default new Vuex.Store({
```

```
  modules: {
    countStore,
  },
});
```

Our `App.vue` then changes slightly; instead of referencing the types object, we reference the types specifically from this module:

```
import * as fromCount from './store/modules/count';

export default {
  data() {
    return {
      amount: 0,
    };
  },
  methods: {
    increment() {
      this.$store.dispatch(fromCount.INCREMENT, this.getAmount);
    },
    decrement() {
      this.$store.dispatch(fromCount.DECREMENT, this.getAmount);
    },
    reset() {
      this.$store.dispatch(fromCount.RESET);
    },
  },
  computed: {
    count() {
      return this.$store.getters.count;
    },
    getAmount() {
      return Number(this.amount) || 1;
    },
  },
};
```

We can then add more modules to our application by having the same files/structure as our count example. This allows us to scale as our application continues to grow.

Summary

In this chapter, we took advantage of the Vuex library for consistent state management within Vue. We defined what state is as well as component state and application-level state. We learned how to appropriately split our actions, getters, mutations, and store between different files for scalability as well as how to call these items within our components.

We also looked at using the Vue devtools with Vuex to step through mutations as they happened within our application. This gives us the ability to better debug/reason about the decisions we make when developing applications.

In the next chapter, we'll look at testing our Vue applications and how to let our tests drive our component design.

10
Testing Vue.js Applications

In a world with tight deadliness and accelerating requirements, creating automated tests for our applications becomes more important than ever. An important factor to consider, which most developers overlook, is the fact that testing is a skill, and just because you may be comfortable coding up solutions, it doesn't automatically mean that you can write good unit tests. As you get more experience in this area, you'll find yourself writing tests more often and wonder what you ever did without them!

By the end of this chapter, we will cover the following:

- Learning about why you should consider using automated testing tools and techniques
- Writing your first unit test for Vue components
- Writing tests that mock out particular functions
- Writing tests that are dependent on Vue.js events
- Using Wallaby.js to see the results of our tests in real time

When we talk about testing our Vue projects, we can mean different things, depending on the context.

Why testing?

Automated testing tools exist for a reason. When it comes to testing the work that we've created manually, you'll know from experience that this is a long, (sometimes complex) process that does not allow for consistent results. Not only do we have to manually remember whether a particular component works (or otherwise write the results down somewhere!), but it isn't resilient to change.

Here are some phrases I've heard over the years when testing has been brought up:

"But Paul, if I write tests for my application it'll take three times as long!"

"I don't know how to write tests..."

"That's not my job!"

...and a variety of others.

The point is that testing is a skill in the same sense that development is a skill. You may not be immediately great at one or the other, but with time, practice, and perseverance, you should find yourself in a position where testing feels natural and a normal part of software development.

Unit testing

Automated testing tools take the manual work we'd be doing each time we want to verify that our feature works as expected, and give us a way to run a command that tests our assertions one by one. This is then shown to us in reports (or live in our editor, as we'll see later on), which gives us the ability to refactor code that isn't working as intended.

By using automated testing tools, we're saving ourselves a vast amount of effort when compared to manual testing.

Unit testing can be defined as a type of testing that only tests one "unit" (the smallest testable part of a feature) at a time. We can then automate this process to continually test our features as the application gets larger. At this point, you may wish to follow Test-Driven Development/Behavior Driven-Development practices.

In the modern JavaScript testing ecosystem, there are a variety of test suites available. These test suites can be thought of as applications that give us the ability to write assertions, run our tests, provide us with coverage reports, and much more. We'll be using Jest inside our project, as this is a fast and flexible suite created and maintained by Facebook.

Let's create a new playground project so that we can get familiar with Unit testing. We'll be using the `webpack` template instead of the `webpack-simple` template, as this allows us to configure testing by default:

```
# Create a new Vue project
$ vue init webpack vue-testing

? Project name vue-testing
```

```
? Project description Various examples of testing Vue.js applications
? Author Paul Halliday <hello@paulhalliday.io>
? Vue build runtime
? Install vue-router? Yes
? Use ESLint to lint your code? Yes
? Pick an ESLint preset Airbnb
? Set up unit tests Yes
? Pick a test runner jest
? Setup e2e tests with Nightwatch? No
? Should we run `npm install` for you after the project has been create
d? (recommended) npm

# Navigate to directory
$ cd vue-testing

# Run application
$ npm run dev
```

Let's start off by investigating the `test/unit/specs` directory. This is where we'll be placing all of our unit/integration tests when testing our Vue components. Open up `HelloWorld.spec.js`, and let's go through it line by line:

```
// Importing Vue and the HelloWorld component
import Vue from 'vue';
import HelloWorld from '@/components/HelloWorld';

// 'describe' is a function used to define the 'suite' of tests
(i.e.overall context).
describe('HelloWorld.vue', () => {

  //'it' is a function that allows us to make assertions (i.e. test
  true/false)
  it('should render correct contents', () => {
    // Create a sub class of Vue based on our HelloWorld component
    const Constructor = Vue.extend(HelloWorld);

    // Mount the component onto a Vue instance
    const vm = new Constructor().$mount();

    // The h1 with the 'hello' class' text should equal 'Welcome to
    Your Vue.js App'
    expect(vm.$el.querySelector('.hello h1').textContent).toEqual(
      'Welcome to Your Vue.js App',
    );
  });
});
```

We can then run these tests by running `npm run unit` inside our Terminal (ensure that you're in the project directory). This will then tell us how many tests have passed as well as the overall test code coverage. This metric can be used as a way to determine how robust an application is in 60; most circumstances; however, it should not be used as gospel. In the following screenshot, we can clearly see how many of our tests have passed:

Setting up vue-test-utils

For a better testing experience, it's advised to use the `vue-test-utils` module as this provides us with many helpers and patterns that are exclusively used with the Vue framework. Let's create a new project based on the `webpack-simple` template and integrate Jest and `vue-test-utils` ourselves. Run the following in your Terminal:

```
# Create a new Vue project
$ vue init webpack-simple vue-test-jest

# Navigate to directory
$ cd vue-test-jest
```

```
# Install dependencies
$ npm install

# Install Jest and vue-test-utils
$ npm install jest vue-test-utils --save-dev

# Run application
$ npm run dev
```

Then, we have to add some extra configuration to our project so that we can run Jest, our test suite. This can be configured inside our project's `package.json`. Add the following:

```
{
  "scripts": {
    "test": "jest"
  }
}
```

This means that any time we want to run our tests, we simply run `npm run test` inside our Terminal. This runs the local (project installed) version of Jest on any files that match the `*.spec.js` name.

Next, we need to tell Jest how to handle Single File Components (that is, `*.vue` files) within our project. This requires the `vue-jest` preprocessor. We'll also want to use ES2015+ syntax inside of our tests, so we'll also need the `babel-jest` preprocessor. Let's install both by running the following in the Terminal:

```
npm install --save-dev babel-jest vue-jest
```

We can then define the following object inside `package.json`:

```
"jest": {
  "moduleNameMapper": {
    "^@/(.*)$": "<rootDir>/src/$1"
  },
  "moduleFileExtensions": [
    "js",
    "vue"
  ],
  "transform": {
    "^.+\\.js$": "<rootDir>/node_modules/babel-jest",
    ".*\\.(vue)$": "<rootDir>/node_modules/vue-jest"
  }
}
```

This is essentially telling Jest how to handle both JavaScript and Vue files, by knowing which preprocessor to use (that is, `babel-jest` or `vue-jest`), depending on the context.

We can also make our tests run quicker if we tell Babel to only transpile features for the Node version we're currently loading. Let's add a separate test environment to our `.babelrc` file:

```
{
  "presets": [["env", { "modules": false }], "stage-3"],
  "env": {
    "test": {
      "presets": [["env", { "targets": { "node": "current" } }]]
    }
  }
}
```

Now that we've added the appropriate configuration, let's start testing!

Creating a TodoList

Let's now create a `TodoList.vue` component inside `src/components` folder. This is the component that we will be testing, and we'll slowly add more features to it:

```
<template>
  <div>
    <h1>Todo List</h1>
    <ul>
      <li v-for="todo in todos" v-bind:key="todo.id">
        {{todo.id}}. {{todo.name}}</li>
    </ul>
  </div>
</template>

<script>
export default {
  data() {
    return {
      todos: [
        { id: 1, name: 'Wash the dishes' },
        { id: 2, name: 'Clean the car' },
        { id: 3, name: 'Learn about Vue.js' },
      ],
    };
  },
};
```

```
</script>

<style>
ul,
li {
  list-style: none;
  margin-left: 0;
  padding-left: 0;
}
</style>
```

As you can see, we just have a simple application that returns an array of to-dos with varying items. Let's create a router inside src/router/index.js to match our new TodoList component and display it as the root:

```
import Vue from 'vue';
import Router from 'vue-router';
import TodoList from '../components/TodoList';

Vue.use(Router);

export default new Router({
  routes: [
    {
      path: '/',
      name: 'TodoList',
      component: TodoList,
    },
  ],
});
```

As we're using vue-router, we'll also need to install it. Run the following in your Terminal:

```
$ npm install vue-router --save-dev
```

We can then add the router to main.js:

```
import Vue from 'vue'
import App from './App.vue'
import router from './router';

new Vue({
  el: '#app',
  router,
  render: h => h(App)
})
```

I've now added `router-view` and elected to remove the Vue logo from `App.vue`, so we have a cleaner user interface. Here's the template for `App.vue`:

```
<template>
  <div id="app">
    <router-view/>
  </div>
</template>
```

As we can see in our browser, it displays our template with the name of **TodoList** and the `todo` items we created as well:

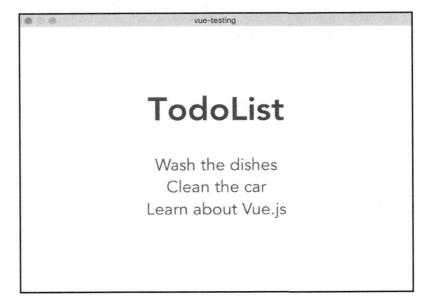

Let's write some tests for this component

Writing tests

Inside the `src/components` folder, make a new folder named `__tests__` and then create a file named `TodoList.spec.js`. Jest will automatically find this folder and subsequent tests.

Let's first import our component and the `mount` method from the test utilities:

```
import { mount } from 'vue-test-utils';
import TodoList from '../TodoList';
```

The `mount` method allows us to test our `TodoList` component in isolation and gives us the ability to mock any input props, events, and even outputs. Next, let's create a describe block that we'll use to contain our test suite:

```
describe('TodoList.vue', () => {

});
```

Let's now mount the component and gain access to the Vue instance:

```
describe('TodoList.vue', () => {
  // Vue instance can be accessed at wrapper.vm
  const wrapper = mount(TodoList);
});
```

Next, we need to define the `it` block to assert the outcome of our test case. Let's make our first expectation—it should render a list of to-do items:

```
describe('TodoList.vue', () => {
  const todos = [{ id: 1, name: 'Wash the dishes' }];
  const wrapper = mount(TodoList);

  it('should contain a list of Todo items', () => {
    expect(wrapper.vm.todos).toContainEqual(todos[0]);
  });
});
```

We can watch changes for our tests by running `$ npm run test -- --watchAll` in the Terminal. Alternatively, we can make a new script inside `package.json` that does this for us:

```
"scripts": {
  "test:watch": "jest --watchAll"
}
```

Now, if we run `npm run test:watch` inside of the Terminal, it will watch the filesystem for any changes.

Here are our results:

```
Pauls-iMac:vue-test-jest paulhalliday$ npm test

> vue-test-jest@1.0.0 test /Users/paulhalliday/vuej
est
> jest

 PASS  src/components/__test__/TodoList.spec.js
  TodoList.vue
    ✓ should contain a list of Todo items (7ms)


Test Suites: 1 passed, 1 total
Tests:       1 passed, 1 total
Snapshots:   0 total
Time:        3.935s, estimated 5s
Ran all test suites.
Pauls-iMac:vue-test-jest paulhalliday$ ▊
```

That's interesting. We have a passing test! However, we have to think to ourselves at this point, is this test brittle? In a real-world application, we may not have items inside our `TodoList` at runtime by default.

We need a way to set properties on our isolated tests. This is where the ability to set our own Vue options comes in handy!

Vue options

We can set our own options on a Vue instance. Let's use `vue-test-utils` to set our own data on the instance and see whether this data is being rendered on screen:

```
describe('TodoList.vue', () => {
  it('should contain a list of Todo items', () => {
    const todos = [{ id: 1, name: 'Wash the dishes' }];
    const wrapper = mount(TodoList, {
      data: { todos },
    });
```

```
    // Find the list items on the page
    const liWrapper = wrapper.find('li').text();

    // List items should match the todos item in data
    expect(liWrapper).toBe(todos[0].name);
  });
});
```

As we can see, we're now testing against the items rendered on the screen based on the data option within our component.

Let's add a `TodoItem` component so that we can render a component with a `todo` prop dynamically. We can then test this component's output based on our prop:

```
<template>
  <li>{{todo.name}}</li>
</template>

<script>
export default {
  props: ['todo'],
};
</script>
```

We can then add it to the `TodoList` component:

```
<template>
  <div>
    <h1>TodoList</h1>
    <ul>
      <TodoItem v-for="todo in todos" v-bind:key="todo.id"
      :todo="todo">{{todo.name}}</TodoItem>
    </ul>
  </div>
</template>

<script>
import TodoItem from './TodoItem';

export default {
  components: {
    TodoItem,
  },
  // Omitted
}
```

Our tests still pass as expected, because the component is rendered into `li` at runtime. It may be a better idea to change this to find the component itself though:

```
import { mount } from 'vue-test-utils';
import TodoList from '../TodoList';
import TodoItem from '../TodoItem';

describe('TodoList.vue', () => {
  it('should contain a list of Todo items', () => {
    const todos = [{ id: 1, name: 'Wash the dishes' }];
    const wrapper = mount(TodoList, {
      data: { todos },
    });

    // Find the list items on the page
    const liWrapper = wrapper.find(TodoItem).text();

    // List items should match the todos item in data
    expect(liWrapper).toBe(todos[0].name);
  });
});
```

Let's write some tests for our `TodoItem` and create a `TodoItem.spec.js` inside `components/__tests__`:

```
import { mount } from 'vue-test-utils';
import TodoItem from '../TodoItem';

describe('TodoItem.vue', () => {
  it('should display name of the todo item', () => {
    const todo = { id: 1, name: 'Wash the dishes' };
    const wrapper = mount(TodoItem, { propsData: { todo } });

    // Find the list items on the page
    const liWrapper = wrapper.find('li').text();

    // List items should match the todos item in data
    expect(liWrapper).toBe(todo.name);
  });
});
```

As we're essentially using the same logic, our test is similar. The main difference is that instead of having a list of `todos`, we just have one `todo` object. We're mocking the props with `propsData` instead of data, essentially asserting that we can add properties to this component and it renders the correct data. Let's take a look at whether our tests passed or failed:

```
> vue-test-jest@1.0.0 test /Users/paulhalliday/vue
js-book/chapter-10/vue-test-jest
> jest


 PASS  src/components/__test__/TodoItem.spec.js (5
.616s)
 PASS  src/components/__test__/TodoList.spec.js (5
.63s)

Test Suites: 2 passed, 2 total
Tests:       2 passed, 2 total
Snapshots:   0 total
Time:        10.959s
Ran all test suites.
Pauls-iMac:vue-test-jest paulhalliday$
```

Adding new features

Let's take a test-driven approach to adding new features to our application. We'll need a way to add new items to our `todo` list, so let's start by writing our tests first. Inside `TodoList.spec.js`, we'll add another `it` assertion that should add an item to our `todo` list:

```
it('should add an item to the todo list', () => {
  const wrapper = mount(TodoList);
  const todos = wrapper.vm.todos;
  const newTodos = wrapper.vm.addTodo('Go to work');
  expect(todos.length).toBeLessThan(newTodos.length);
});
```

If we run our tests right now, we'll get a failing test this is expected!:

```
●●●                    Shell                    Shell                    Shell

FAIL  src/components/__test__/TodoList.spec.js
  ● TodoList.vue > should add an item to the todo list

    TypeError: wrapper.vm.addTodo is not a function

      20 |        const wrapper = mount(TodoList);
      21 |        const todos = wrapper.vm.todos;
    > 22 |        const newTodos = wrapper.vm.addTodo('Go
 to work');
      23 |
      24 |        expect(todos.length).toBeLessThan(newTo
 dos.length);
      25 |    });

      at Object.<anonymous> (src/components/__test__/T
 odoList.spec.js:22:31)

 ~/vuejs-book/chapter-10/vue-test-jest
```

Let's do the minimum possible to fix our error. We can add a method named `addTodo` inside our Vue instance:

```
export default {
  methods: {
    addTodo(name) {},
  },
  // Omitted
}
```

Now we get a new error; this time, it states that it **Cannot read property 'length' of undefined**, essentially saying that we have no `newTodos` array:

```
FAIL  src/components/__test__/TodoList.spec.js
  ● TodoList.vue > should add an item to the todo list

    TypeError: Cannot read property 'length' of undefined

      22 |        const newTodos = wrapper.vm.addTodo('Go to w
    ork');
      23 |
    > 24 |        expect(todos.length).toBeLessThan(newTodos.l
    ength);
      25 |    });
      26 |  });
      27 |

      at Object.<anonymous> (src/components/__test__/TodoLi
```

Let's make our `addTodo` function return an array that combines the current `todos` with a new todo:

```
addTodo(name) {
  return [...this.todos, { name }]
},
```

We get this output after running `npm test`:

```
Pauls-iMac:vue-test-jest paulhalliday$ npm test

> vue-test-jest@1.0.0 test /Users/paulhalliday/vuejs-book/c
hapter-10/vue-test-jest
> jest

 PASS  src/components/__test__/TodoItem.spec.js
 PASS  src/components/__test__/TodoList.spec.js

Test Suites: 2 passed, 2 total
Tests:       3 passed, 3 total
Snapshots:   0 total
Time:        4.486s, estimated 7s
Ran all test suites.
Pauls-iMac:vue-test-jest paulhalliday$
```

Ta-da! Passing tests.

Hmm. I do remember all of our `todo` items having an appropriate `id`, but it looks like that's no longer the case.

Ideally, our server-side database should handle `id` numbers for us, but for now, we can work with a client-side generated `uuid` using the `uuid` package. Let's install it by running the following in the Terminal:

```
$ npm install uuid
```

We can then write our test case to assert that each item added to the list has an `id` property:

```
it('should add an id to each todo item', () => {
  const wrapper = mount(TodoList);
  const todos = wrapper.vm.todos;
  const newTodos = wrapper.vm.addTodo('Go to work');

  newTodos.map(item => {
    expect(item.id).toBeTruthy();
  });
});
```

As you can see, the Terminal outputs that we have an issue, and this is caused because we evidently don't have an `id` property:

Let's use the `uuid` package we installed earlier to achieve this goal:

```
import uuid from 'uuid/v4';

export default {
  methods: {
    addTodo(name) {
      return [...this.todos, { id: uuid(), name }];
    },
  },
  // Omitted
};
```

We then get a passing test:

```
Pauls-iMac:vue-test-jest paulhalliday$ npm test

> vue-test-jest@1.0.0 test /Users/paulhalliday/vuejs-book/c
hapter-10/vue-test-jest
> jest

PASS  src/components/__test__/TodoList.spec.js
PASS  src/components/__test__/TodoItem.spec.js

Test Suites: 2 passed, 2 total
Tests:       4 passed, 4 total
Snapshots:   0 total
Time:        0.839s, estimated 1s
Ran all test suites.
Pauls-iMac:vue-test-jest paulhalliday$
```

Starting off with a failing test is beneficial for multiple reasons:

- It ensures that our test is actually running and we don't spend time debugging anything!
- We know what we need to implement next, as we're driven by the current error message

We can then write the minimum necessary to get a green test and continue to refactor our code until we're satisfied with our solution. In the previous tests, we could have written even less to get a green result, but for brevity, I've elected for smaller examples.

Click events

Great! Our method works, but that's not how our user will be interacting with the application. Let's see whether we can make our tests take into account a user input form and subsequent button:

```
<form @submit.prevent="addTodo(todoName)">
  <input type="text" v-model="todoName">
  <button type="submit">Submit</button>
</form>
```

We can also make a small change to our `addTodo` function, ensuring that `this.todos` is given the value of the new `todo` items:

```
addTodo(name) {
  this.todos = [...this.todos, { id: uuid(), name }];
  return this.todos;
},
```

The great thing is that by making this change, we can check against all of our previous use cases and see that nothing fails! Hurray for automated testing!

Next, let's make an `it` block that we can use to assert that whenever our **Submit** button is clicked on, an item is added:

```
it('should add an item to the todo list when the button is clicked', ()
=> {
   const wrapper = mount(TodoList);
})
```

Next, we can get the form element from within the wrapper using find, and this allows us to then trigger an event. As we're submitting a form, we'll trigger the submit event and pass along a parameter to our `submit` function. We can then assert that our `todo` list should be 1:

```
it('should add an item to the todo list when the button is clicked', () =>
{
 const wrapper = mount(TodoList);
 wrapper.find('form').trigger('submit', 'Clean the car');

 const todos = wrapper.vm.todos;

 expect(todos.length).toBe(1);
})
```

We can also check to see whether the appropriate method was called when the form is submitted. Let's do that using `jest`:

```
it('should call addTodo when form is submitted', () => {
  const wrapper = mount(TodoList);
  const spy = jest.spyOn(wrapper.vm, 'addTodo');
  wrapper.find('form').trigger('submit', 'Clean the car');

  expect(wrapper.vm.addTodo).toHaveBeenCalled();
});
```

Testing events

We've made a lot of progress, but wouldn't it be great if we could test events that fire between components? Let's take a look at this by creating a `TodoInput`, component and abstracting our form away into `this` component:

```
<template>
  <form @submit.prevent="addTodo(todoName)">
    <input type="text" v-model="todoName">
    <button type="submit">Submit</button>
  </form>
</template>

<script>
export default {
  data() {
    return {
      todoName: ''
    }
  },
  methods: {
    addTodo(name) {
      this.$emit('addTodo', name);
    }
  }
}
</script>
```

Now, our `addTodo` method inside of `this` component fires an event. Let's test that event within a `TodoInput.spec.js` file:

```
import { mount } from 'vue-test-utils';
import TodoInput from '../TodoInput';

describe('TodoInput.vue', () => {
  it('should fire an event named addTodo with todo name', () => {
    const mock = jest.fn()
    const wrapper = mount(TodoInput);

    wrapper.vm.$on('addTodo', mock)
    wrapper.vm.addTodo('Clean the car');

    expect(mock).toBeCalledWith('Clean the car')
  })
});
```

We're introduced to a new concept inside of this method—mock. This allows us to define our own behavior and subsequently determine what the event was called with.

Whenever the addTodo event is fired, the mock function is called instead. This allows us to see whether our event is being called and also ensures that the event can take a payload.

We can also ensure that the TodoList handles this event, but firstly, ensure that you've updated the TodoList to include the TodoInput form:

```
<template>
  <div>
    <h1>TodoList</h1>

    <TodoInput @addTodo="addTodo($event)"></TodoInput>

    <ul>
      <TodoItem v-for="todo in todos" v-bind:key="todo.id"
:todo="todo">{{todo.name}}</TodoItem>
    </ul>
  </div>
</template>

<script>
import uuid from 'uuid/v4';

import TodoItem from './TodoItem';
import TodoInput from './TodoInput';

export default {
  components: {
    TodoItem,
    TodoInput
  },
  data() {
    return {
      todos: [],
      todoName: ''
    };
  },
  methods: {
    addTodo(name) {
      this.todos = [...this.todos, { id: uuid(), name }];
      return this.todos;
    },
  },
};
</script>
```

```
<style>
ul,
li {
  list-style: none;
  margin-left: 0;
  padding-left: 0;
}
</style>
```

Then, inside our `TodoList.spec.js`, we can start off by importing `TodoInput` and then add the following:

```
import TodoInput from '../TodoInput';
it('should call addTodo when the addTodo event happens', () => {
  const wrapper = mount(TodoList);
  wrapper.vm.addTodo = jest.fn();
  wrapper.find(TodoInput).vm.$emit('addTodo', 'Clean the car');

  expect(wrapper.vm.addTodo).toBeCalledWith('Clean the car');
})
```

Apart from that, we can also ensure that the event does what it's supposed to do; so when we fire the event it adds an item to the array and we are testing for the array length:

```
it('adds an item to the todolist when the addTodo event happens', () => {
  const wrapper = mount(TodoList);
  wrapper.find(TodoInput).vm.$emit('addTodo', 'Clean the car');
  const todos = wrapper.vm.todos;
  expect(todos.length).toBe(1);
});
```

Using Wallaby.js for a better testing experience

We can also use Wallaby.js to see the results of our unit tests in real time within our editor. It's not a free tool, but you may find it useful when creating test-driven Vue applications. Let's start off by cloning/downloading a project that already has Wallaby set up. Run the following in your Terminal:

```
# Clone the repository
$ git clone https://github.com/ChangJoo-Park/vue-wallaby-webpack-template

# Change directory
$ cd vue-wallaby-webpack-template
```

```
# Install dependencies
$ npm install

# At the time of writing this package is missing eslint-plugin-node
$ npm install eslint-plugin-node

# Run in browser
$ npm run dev
```

We can then open this up inside our editor and install the **Wallaby.js** extension inside our editor. You can find a list of supported editors and instructions at `https://wallabyjs.com/download/`.

I'll be installing this within Visual Studio Code, which starts by searching the extensions marketplace for Wallaby:

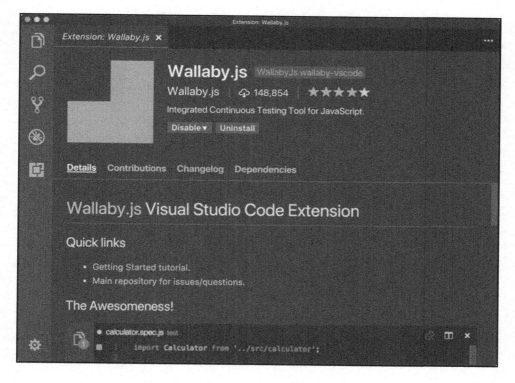

We can then tell Wallaby about the project's configuration file (`wallaby.js`), by pressing *CMD + SHIFT + =* on Mac or *CTRL + SHIFT + =* on Windows. From the drop-down, click on **Select Configuration File** and subsequently, type `wallaby.js`. This will allow Wallaby and Vue to work together.

To start Wallaby, we can open the configuration menu again and select **Start**. We can then navigate to the `tests/unit/specs/Hello.spec.js` file, and we should see varying blocks in the line margins of the editor:

```js
import Vue from 'vue'
import Hello from '@/components/Hello'

describe('Hello.vue', () => {
  // Scenario 1: Check text content
  it('should render correct contents', () => {    83ms
    const Constructor = Vue.extend(Hello)
    const vm = new Constructor().$mount()
    expect(vm.$el.querySelector('.hello h1').textContent)
      .toEqual('Welcome to Your Vue.js App')
  })

  // Scenario 2: Check type of props
  it('should props count is Number', () => {    2ms
    const Constructor = Vue.extend(Hello)
    const vm = new Constructor({
      propsData: { count: 1 }
    }).$mount()
    expect(typeof vm.$props.count).toBe('number')
  })

  // Scenario 3: Check props default value
  it('should props default value of count is 1 ', () => {    2ms
    const Constructor = Vue.extend(Hello)
    const vm = new Constructor().$mount()
    expect(vm.$props.count).toBe(1)
  })
```

As everything is green, we know that it has passed! What if we change the implementation details of the test? Let's purposely make one or more of our tests fail:

Everything stays green apart from the **'should render correct contents'** block, which can be seen down the left-hand side. This is because we now have a failed assertion, but more importantly, we don't have to rerun our tests, and they're displayed instantly within our editor. No more Alt-Tab-ing between different windows to watch our test output!

Summary

This chapter saw us learn about how to appropriately test our Vue components. We learned how to follow the fail-first approach to write tests that drive our development decisions as well as how to take advantage of Wallaby.js to see the results of our tests from within our editor!

In the next chapter, we'll learn how we can combine our Vue.js applications with modern Progressive Web Application techniques, such as service workers, application manifests, and much more!

11
Optimization

If you've been writing applications targeting the web platform for many years, you'll have seen just how many changes the web has gone through. What started off as a simple document viewer now sees us having to deal with complex build steps, state management patterns, continuous review of performance and compatibility, and much more.

Thankfully, the popularity of JavaScript and subsequent tooling means that there are templates and tried-and-tested techniques that we can use to optimize our application and deployment.

In this chapter, we'll take a look at the following topics:

- The `vue-pwa` template from the Vue CLI
- Features of Progressive Web Applications
- Using ngrok to view localhost applications on any device
- Using Firebase hosting to deploy web applications
- Continuous Integration and what it means for large-scale projects
- Automatically running tests on each Git `commit`
- Automatically deploying to Firebase hosting on each Git `commit`

Progressive Web Applications (PWAs)

PWAs can be defined as applications that use the capabilities of the modern web to deliver thoughtful, engaging, and interactive experiences. My definition of PWAs is one that encompasses the principle of progressive enhancement. We could certainly take advantage of everything that PWAs have to offer, but we don't have to (or at least not all at once).

This means that not only are we continuing to improve our application over time, but adhering to these principles forces us to think in the perspective of a user who has bad internet connectivity, wants an offline-first experience, needs home-screen accessible apps, and so on.

Once again, the Vue CLI makes this process easy for us, as it provides a PWA template. Let's create a new Vue application with the appropriate template:

```
# Create a new Vue project
$ vue init pwa vue-pwa

? Project name vue-pwa
? Project short name: fewer than 12 characters to not be truncated on
homescreens (default: same as name)
? Project description A PWA built with Vue.js
? Author Paul Halliday <hello@paulhalliday.io>
? Vue build runtime
? Install vue-router? Yes
? Use ESLint to lint your code? Yes
? Pick an ESLint preset Airbnb
? Setup unit tests with Karma + Mocha? No
? Setup e2e tests with Nightwatch? No

# Navigate to directory
$ cd vue-pwa

# Install dependencies
$ npm install

# Run application
$ npm run dev
```

Throughout this chapter, we'll be looking at the benefits that this template gives us, and ways we can make both our application and operations more progressive.

Web application manifest

You may have seen the benefits of applications that use a web app manifest already—if you've ever been on a website that asks you to install this on your home screen or if you've noticed that the color of the address bar change from default gray to a different color on Android Chrome, that's a progressive app.

Let's head over to `static/manifest.json` and investigate the contents:

```json
{
  "name": "vue-pwa",
  "short_name": "vue-pwa",
  "icons": [
    {
      "src": "/static/img/icons/android-chrome-192x192.png",
      "sizes": "192x192",
      "type": "image/png"
    },
    {
      "src": "/static/img/icons/android-chrome-512x512.png",
      "sizes": "512x512",
      "type": "image/png"
    }
  ],
  "start_url": "/index.html",
  "display": "standalone",
  "background_color": "#000000",
  "theme_color": "#4DBA87"
}
```

We have the option to give our application `name` and `short_name`; these will be shown when installing on the home screen of a device.

The `icons` array is used to provide varying sizes of our icon for a high-definition experience across devices. The `start_url` defines the file to be loaded upon startup when installed on a user's home screen and thus points toward `index.html`.

We can change how our application appears when running on a device as a PWA with the display attribute. There are various options available, such as `browser`, `standalone`, `minimal-ui`, and `fullscreen`. Each one changes how our application is displayed on the device; (https://developers.google.com/web/fundamentals/web-app-manifest/)

here's an example of both browser and standalone:

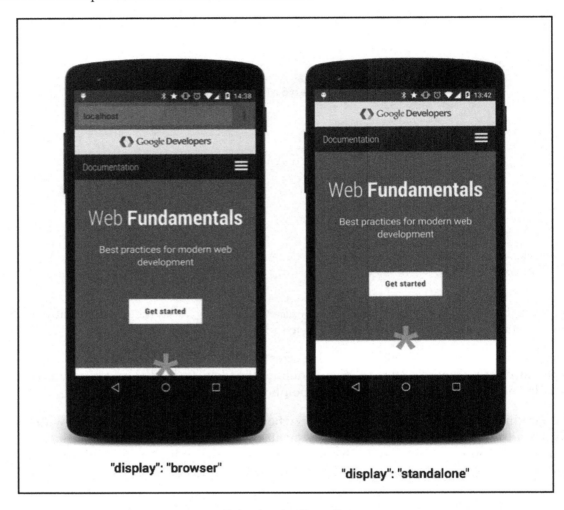

Display options—the web app manifest

We can also take advantage of the `background_color` option to change the color of the splash screen background when our PWA starts, as seen in the following screenshot:

If we want to change the color of the toolbar, we can use the `theme_color` option (we'll look at an example as we move ahead).

There are other options you can pass to your web app manifest and you should customize these based on the needs of your project. You can find more information about the web app manifest on MDN at `https://developer.mozilla.org/en-US/docs/Web/Manifest`.

Testing on a device

If we want to test our application on a device without worrying about deployment, we could use a tool, such as ngrok, to create a tunnel between our localhost and the outside world. This allows us to view our application on any device with a public URL, and once we close the connection, the URL and subsequent application disappear.

Download ngrok by navigating to https://ngrok.com/download and following the installation steps for your platform.

Ngrok also can be installed via npm typing :

```
npm install ngrok -g
```

As our Vue application is running on port 8080, we can start ngrok and tell it to serve from that port. Run the following command in your Terminal with ngrok installed:

```
$ ngrok http 8080
```

We then get the following result in our Terminal:

```
ngrok by @inconshreveable                                    (Ctrl+C to quit)

Session Status           online
Version                  2.2.8
Region                   United States (us)
Web Interface            http://127.0.0.1:4040
Forwarding               http://d2cf75e2.ngrok.io -> localhost:8080
Forwarding               https://d2cf75e2.ngrok.io -> localhost:8080

Connections              ttl     opn     rt1     rt5     p50     p90
                         0       0       0.00    0.00    0.00    0.00
```

We can then navigate to this URL on any device and see the following results on screen:

Isn't this much more of a native experience? Now we have a colored address/status bar by default. We also get access to much more with the power of `ServiceWorker` in production mode. Before we dive into that, let's look at how we can deploy our application to a more permanent URL using Firebase.

Firebase deployment

Firebase is a platform by Google that allows us to take advantage of everything from real-time databases, remote configuration, push notifications, and much more. Perhaps more important for our use case is the potential for static file deployment, and this is something we'll be taking advantage of.

The platform has three different packages available, each offering different levels of service, with the first tier being free and then the following two tiers requiring payment.

Start off by navigating to `https://firebase.google.com` and logging in with a Google account by clicking on **SIGN IN**, and then, click **GO TO CONSOLE** at the top right.

We can then create a new Firebase project by selecting + **Add Project** on the Firebase dashboard and subsequently selecting a project name and country.

We will then navigate to **Project Overview**, where we can choose to add Firebase to our project and a variety of other options. We're looking for hosting, as we're interested in deploying our static content. From the left-side menu, click on **Hosting**:

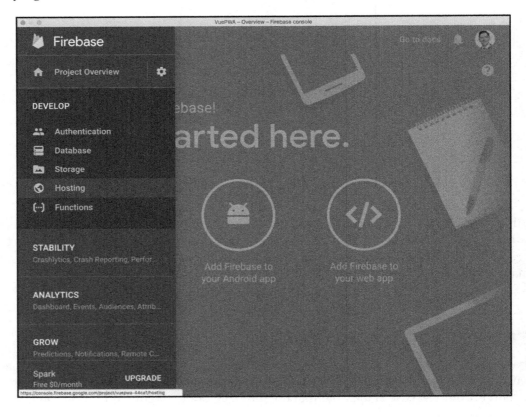

We'll be on this screen quite a bit, as it allows us to revert deployments as well as see other usage metrics. Since we haven't made our first deployment yet, the screen will look similar to this:

If we click on **GET STARTED**, we will receive a message stating that we need to download the Firebase tools. This is a CLI that allows us to manage our Firebase project from within the Terminal.

Install Firebase tools by running the following command in the Terminal:

```
$ npm install firebase-tools -g
```

We can then follow the steps outlined in the next step of the hosting wizard, but we won't be using the deployment step just yet. The wizard should look like the following:

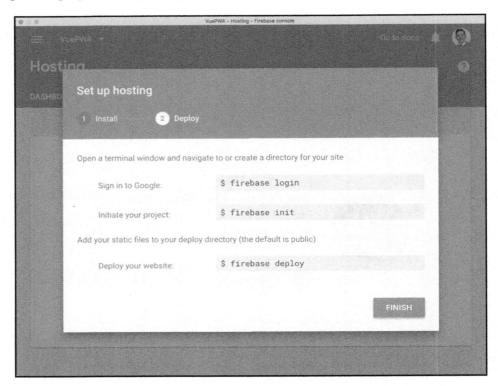

Let's start off by logging in to the Firebase console by running the following in the Terminal:

```
$ firebase login
```

Select a Google account and give it appropriate permissions. You should then be provided the following screen:

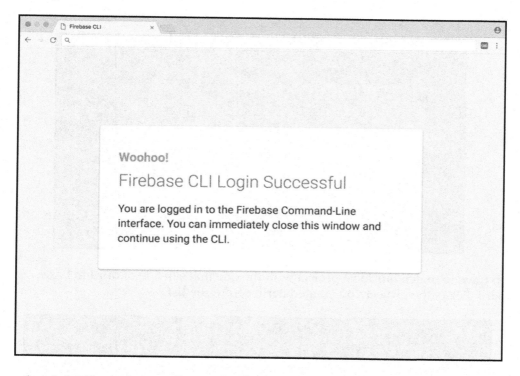

We can then initialize a new Firebase project inside of our `vue-pwa` project. Run the following command in your Terminal:

```
$ firebase init
```

At this point, we can use the keyboard to navigate to hosting and select it with the spacebar. This should make the circle green and it tells Firebase that we'd like to set up hosting within our project.

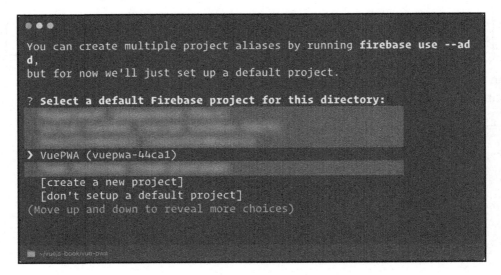

We then have to match our local project with the one that's inside of our Firebase dashboard. Select the project you created earlier from the list:

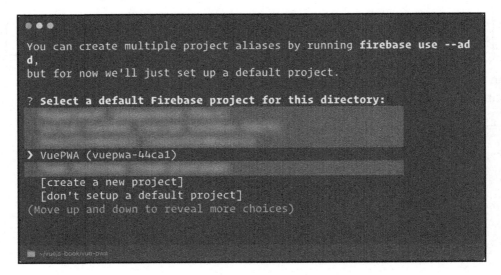

It should then ask you questions related to the setup—answer them like so:

We've now got the ability to deploy to Firebase at will. We'll need to build our project for production to appropriately generate a `dist` folder with the contents of our application. Let's run the following command in the Terminal:

```
$ npm run prod
```

Then, to deploy to Firebase, we can run the following command:

```
$ firebase deploy
```

After a short while, you should be given a navigable URL that contains our application served over HTTPS:

Our Firebase dashboard has also been updated to reflect our deployment:

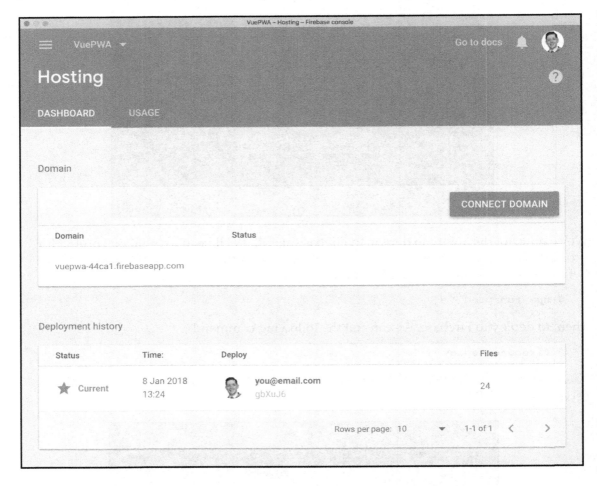

If we then navigate to the URL, we should get our project as expected:

Also, because we built our application using a production build, we can disconnect it from Wi-Fi or check the offline box inside of your Developer Tools. Upon doing so, we will find that our application still runs as expected because we have a `ServiceWorker` running on all production builds.

Continuous Integration (CI)

There are a variety of CI platforms available, such as Travis, GitLab, Jenkins, and countless others. Each platform often serves a common goal, that is, automating deployment and the challenges that come along with it.

Sure, we could deploy our site, run our tests, and continue with other items in our forever increasing build steps. Not only is this a tedious process, but it also gives us many opportunities to make mistakes. Furthermore, it also means that each step has to be documented for every member of the team, the documentation has to be kept up to date and is not exactly scalable across an organization.

For our examples, we'll be using Travis CI, and the first objective that I'd like to tackle is automatically running our unit tests. To do this, we'll need one or more unit tests inside of our project.

Unit tests

We covered testing our Vue.js applications in the preceding chapter, so wouldn't it be nice to automatically run our tests each time we push a new build? Let's quickly set up some tests inside of our project and integrate it with Travis:

```
# Install necessary dependencies
$ npm install jest vue-test-utils babel-jest vue-jest --save-dev
```

We can then add a new script that runs `jest`:

```
{
  "scripts": {
    "test": "jest"
  }
}
```

Next, add the `jest` configuration to your `package.json`:

```
"jest": {
  "moduleNameMapper": {
    "^@/(.*)$": "<rootDir>/src/$1"
  },
  "moduleFileExtensions": [
    "js",
    "vue"
  ],
  "transform": {
    "^.+\\.js$": "<rootDir>/node_modules/babel-jest",
    ".*\\.(vue)$": "<rootDir>/node_modules/vue-jest"
  }
}
```

Finally, we can update our `babel` configuration inside of `.babelrc`:

```
{
  "presets": [
    ["env", {
      "modules": false,
      "targets": {
        "browsers": ["> 1%", "last 2 versions", "not ie <= 8"]
      }
    }],
    "stage-2"
  ],
  "plugins": ["transform-runtime"],
  "env": {
    "test": {
      "presets": [["env", { "targets": { "node": "current" } }]],
      "plugins": [ "istanbul" ]
    }
  }
}
```

We can then make a sample test inside of `components/__test__/Hello.spec.js` that simply checks whether `msg` inside of our data matches a string:

```
import { mount } from 'vue-test-utils';
import Hello from '../Hello';

describe('Hello.vue', () => {
  it('should greet the user', () => {
    const wrapper = mount(Hello);

    expect(wrapper.vm.msg).toEqual('Welcome to Your Vue.js PWA');
  })
})
```

As expected, we can then run `npm test` to execute our tests:

```
Pauls-iMac:vue-pwa paulhalliday$ npm test

> vue-pwa@1.0.0 test /Users/paulhalliday/vuej
s-book/vue-pwa
> jest

 PASS  src/components/__tests__/Hello.spec.js
  Hello.vue
    ✓ should greet the user (13ms)


Test Suites: 1 passed, 1 total
Tests:       1 passed, 1 total
Snapshots:   0 total
Time:        0.884s
Ran all test suites.
Pauls-iMac:vue-pwa paulhalliday$
```

Creating a Git repository

To use continuous integration with Travis CI, we'll need to upload our project to GitHub. If you haven't already got Git on your machine, download it from `https://git-scm.com/` and subsequently create a GitHub account at `https://github.com`.

Create a new repository for your project at `https://github.com/new`, or by clicking on the **New repository** button by clicking on the **+** at the top-right corner of the screen.

We can then give our repository a name and make the visibility either **Public** or **Private**:

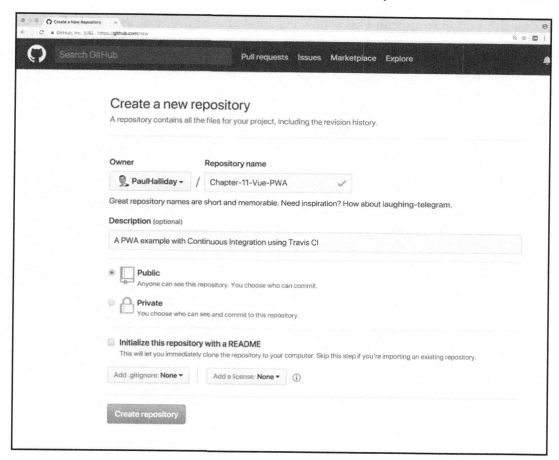

Once we click on the **Create repository** button, we're greeted with a variety of ways in which we can upload our repository to GitHub. The only problem is that we haven't made our PWA project a Git repository yet.

We can do this inside Visual Studio Code or the command line. In Visual Studio Code, click on the **New repository** button. If you've just installed Git, you may need to restart your editor for this button to appear. This is how it should appear inside of Visual Studio Code.

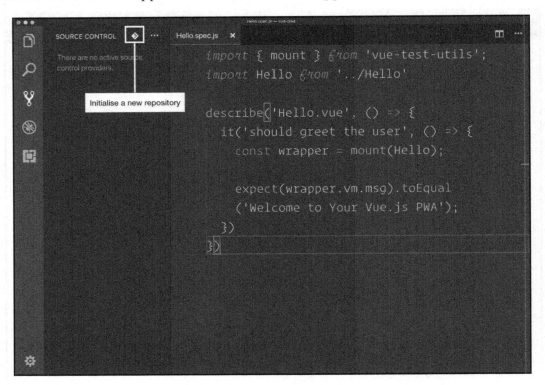

We can then make a new commit with a simple message, such as **First commit**, and subsequently click on the tick:

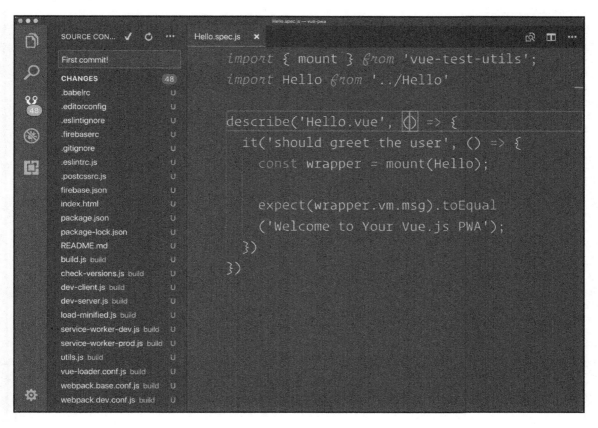

We can then push these changes up to the repository on GitHub by following the steps highlighted inside...or **push an existing repository from the command line** given in the following image:

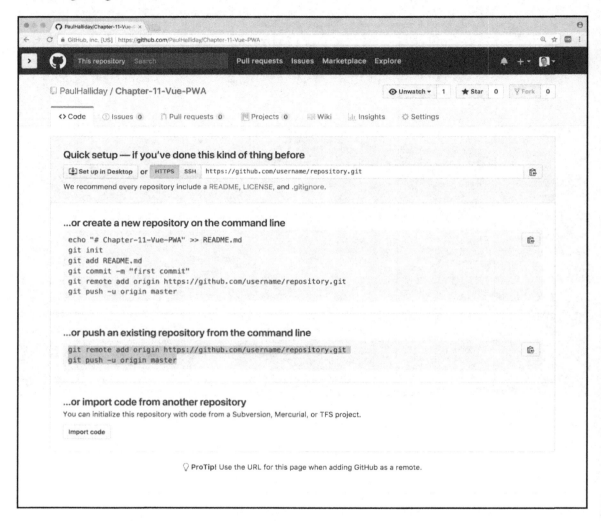

Any future changes to our repository will be pushed to this remote repository. This is important because when we create our Travis account, it'll automatically get access to all of our GitHub repositories.

Connecting to Travis CI

Let's navigate to `https://travis-ci.org/` and click on **Sign in with GitHub.**After giving Travis any necessary permissions, you should then be able to see a list of repositories attached to your account. We can tell Travis that we'd like it to watch for changes in this repository by flicking the switch to green:

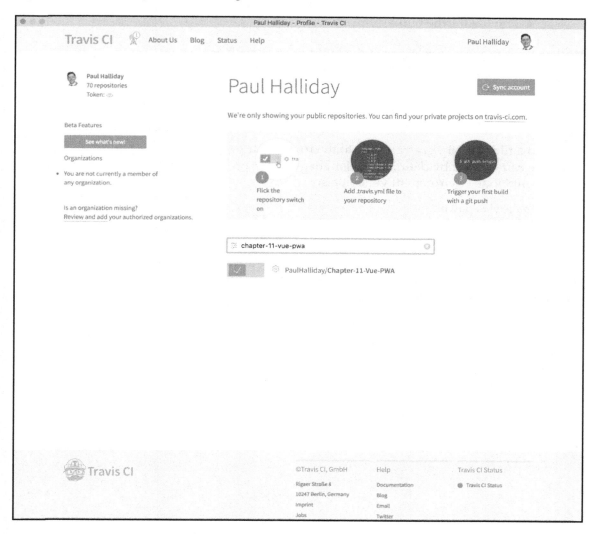

Configuring Travis

The next thing to do is add an appropriate `.travis.yml` configuration file to our project. This will tell Travis what to do each time we push a build to GitHub. As such, there are two distinct phases that happen when we build with Travis:

- Travis installs any dependencies inside of our project
- Travis runs the build script

We can hook into various stages of the build process such as `before_install`, `install`, `before_script`, `script`, `before_cache`, `after_success`, `after_failure`, `before_deploy`, `deploy`, `after_deploy`, and `after_script`. All of these are relatively self-explanatory, but if it seems like a lot to take in—don't worry, we'll only be hooking into a select few of these stages.

Let's add a file named `.travis.yml` to the root of our project and add options one step at a time. We can start off by defining the language of our project and as we're using Node, the subsequent Node environment version also:

```
language: node_js
node_js:
  - "9.3.0"
```

The `node_js` version I've selected matches the same as my environment (this can be checked with `node -v`), but if you need to target a specific version of Node (or more than one version), you can add them here.

Next, let's add that we'd only like to trigger builds on the `master` branch:

```
branches:
  only:
    - master
```

Then, we will need to tell Travis what script to run from `package.json`. As we'd like to run our tests, we'll be running the test script:

```
script:
  - npm run test
```

Finally, let's state that we'd like to receive email notifications for every build:

```
notifications:
  email:
    recipients:
      - your@email.com
    on_success: always
    on_failure: always
```

This gives us the following file:

```
language: node_js
node_js:
  - "9.3.0"

branches:
  only:
    - master

script:
  - npm run build
  - npm run test

notifications:
  email:
    recipients:
      - your@email.com
    on_success: always
    on_failure: always
```

If we then push these changes to our repository and sync it with the origin, we should be able to watch our Travis console as it runs our tests. It may take a few minutes for Travis to start the build as follows, so be patient:

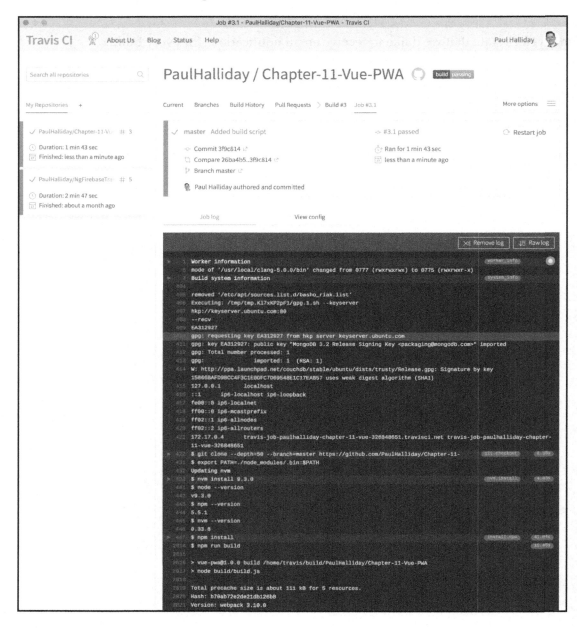

If we scroll down to the bottom of the log, you can see that our project was built for both productions and our tests run:

```
2861    PASS  src/components/__tests__/Hello.spec.js
2862      Hello.vue
2863        ✓ should greet the user (41ms)
2864
2865    Test Suites: 1 passed, 1 total
2866    Tests:       1 passed, 1 total
2867    Snapshots:   0 total
2868    Time:        2.583s
2869    Ran all test suites.
```

Awesome! We can now run our tests and hook into various stages of the build process with Travis CI. Given that we're building our project for production on Travis, we should be able to deploy this build to Firebase automatically.

Let's change our `Hello.vue` component to have a new message (and also make our test fail):

```
export default {
  name: 'hello',
  data() {
    return {
      msg: 'Welcome to Your Vue.js PWA! Deployed to Firebase by Travis CI',
    };
  },
};
```

Automatic deployment to Firebase

We can let Travis handle our deployment automatically, but we'll need a way to give Travis access to our deployment token. We can get this token for CI environments by running the following command in the Terminal:

```
$ firebase login:ci
```

After logging in to your Google account once again, you should be given a token inside of the Terminal:

✔ **Success! Use this token to login on a CI server:**

 # Token here

Keep the token for now, as we'll need it in a second.

Navigate back to the **Travis CI** dashboard, and go to the settings for your project. Inside of the settings, we'll need to add an environment variable that we can then reference inside of our deployment script.

Add the `FIREBASE_TOKEN` environment variable with the value equal to the token we got from the Terminal:

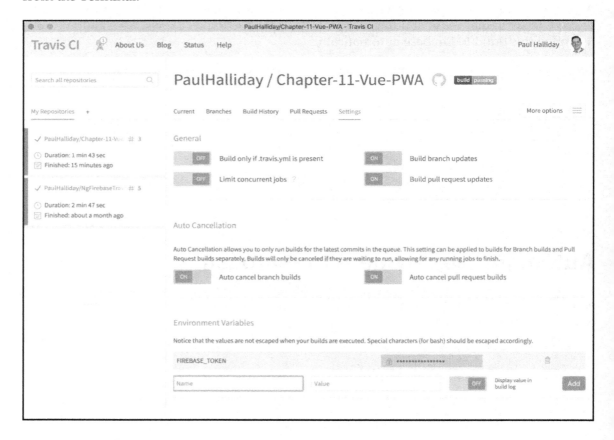

We can then update our `.travis.yml` file to install the firebase tools in our CI environment, and if everything is successful, then deploy them to our Firebase hosting environment:

```
language: node_js
node_js:
  - "9.3.0"

branches:
  only:
    - master

before_script:
  - npm install -g firebase-tools

script:
  - npm run build
  - npm run test

after_success:
  - firebase deploy --token $FIREBASE_TOKEN

notifications:
  email:
    recipients:
      - your@email.com
    on_success: always
    on_failure: always
```

Make a new commit after changing this file and sync the repositories. This should then trigger a new build on Travis, and we can watch for the log.

Here are the results:

```
2906  FAIL src/components/__tests__/Hello.spec.js
2907    Hello.vue
2908      × should greet the user (41ms)
2909
2910    ● Hello.vue › should greet the user
2911
2912      expect(received).toEqual(expected)
2913
2914      Expected value to equal:
2915        "Welcome to Your Vue.js PWA"
2916      Received:
2917        "Welcome to Your Vue.js PWA! Deployed to Firebase by Travis CI"
2918
2919        6 |      const wrapper = mount(Hello);
2920        7 |
2921      > 8 |      expect(wrapper.vm.msg).toEqual('Welcome to Your Vue.js PWA');
2922        9 |    })
2923       10 | })
2924
2925        at Object.<anonymous> (src/components/__tests__/Hello.spec.js:8:28)
2926
2927  Test Suites: 1 failed, 1 total
2928  Tests:       1 failed, 1 total
2929  Snapshots:   0 total
2930  Time:        2.03s
2931  Ran all test suites.
2932  npm ERR! code ELIFECYCLE
2933  npm ERR! errno 1
2934  npm ERR! vue-pwa@1.0.0 test: `jest`
2935  npm ERR! Exit status 1
2936  npm ERR!
2937  npm ERR! Failed at the vue-pwa@1.0.0 test script.
2938  npm ERR! This is probably not a problem with npm. There is likely additional logging output above.
2939
2940  npm ERR! A complete log of this run can be found in:
2941  npm ERR!     /home/travis/.npm/_logs/2018-01-09T15_27_53_984Z-debug.log
2942
2943
2944  The command "npm run test" exited with 1.
```

Our deployment failed **because our test(s) failed.** Note how our application hosted on Firebase didn't change at all. This is intended and is why we placed the deployment step inside `after_success` because if we have failing tests, we most likely don't want to be pushing this code to production.

Let's fix our test(s) and push a new `commit` to the repository:

```
import { mount } from 'vue-test-utils';
import Hello from '../Hello'

describe('Hello.vue', () => {
  it('should greet the user', () => {
    const wrapper = mount(Hello);

    expect(wrapper.vm.msg).toEqual('Welcome to Your Vue.js PWA! Deployed to
Firebase by Travis CI');
  })
})
```

As all of our scripts passed with an exit code of 0 (no errors), the `after_success` hook was fired, pushing our project to Firebase Hosting:

```
2900  The command "npm run build" exited with 0.
2901  $ npm run test
2902
2903  > vue-pwa@1.0.0 test /home/travis/build/PaulHalliday/Chapter-11-Vue-PWA
2904  > jest
2905
2906  PASS src/components/__tests__/Hello.spec.js
2907    Hello.vue
2908      ✓ should greet the user (26ms)
2909
2910  Test Suites: 1 passed, 1 total
2911  Tests:       1 passed, 1 total
2912  Snapshots:   0 total
2913  Time:        1.733s
2914  Ran all test suites.
2915
2916
2917  The command "npm run test" exited with 0.
2918  $ firebase deploy --token $FIREBASE_TOKEN
2931
2932  Done. Your build exited with 0.
```

If we check our application at the appropriate URL, we should see an updated message:

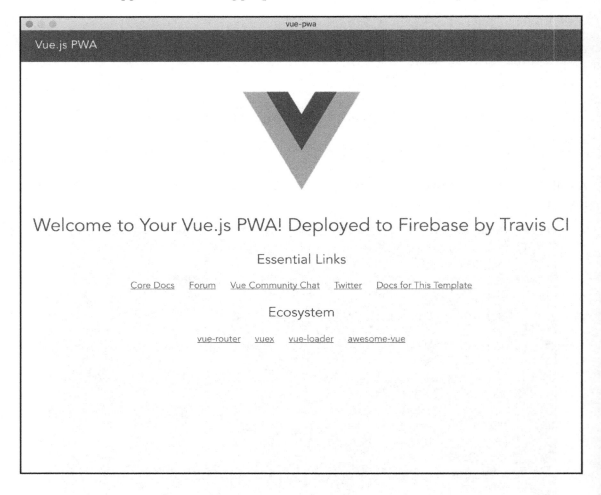

Service worker

When building our application for production using the `vue-pwa` template, it includes `ServiceWorker`. This is essentially a script that runs in the background and allows us to take advantage of offline-first approaches, push notifications, background sync, and more.

Our application will now also prompt our user to install the application on their home screen, as follows:

If we are disconnected from the internet, we'd also get an offline-first experience, as the application still continues to function. This is one of the major benefits we get when using the vue-pwa template, and if you'd like to read more about ServiceWorker and see how you can customize this to your needs, Google has a great onboarding guide at https:// developers.google.com/web/fundamentals/primers/service-workers/.

Summary

In this chapter, we investigated the PWA template from the Vue CLI and subsequently looked at how we can automatically deploy and test our application as it continues to grow. These principles allow us to continually ensure that we can spend more time developing features and less time maintaining deployment documentation and following rudimentary tasks each time.

In the following chapter, we'll cover Nuxt, a framework that allows us to create server-side rendered/static applications using Vue. Nuxt also has an interesting folder-based routing structure, which gives us a lot of power when creating Vue applications.

12
Server-Side Rendering with Nuxt

Nuxt is inspired by a popular React project named Next.js, built by Zeit. Both projects have the aim of creating applications that allow for a better development experience using the latest ideologies, tools, and techniques. Nuxt recently entered version 1.x and onward, meaning that it should be considered stable to use for production websites.

We'll be taking a look at Nuxt in more detail throughout this chapter, and if you find it useful, it may become the default way that you create Vue applications.

In this chapter, we'll cover the following topics:

- Investigating Nuxt and understanding the benefits of using it
- Creating an application with Nuxt
- Using Nuxt middleware
- Using layouts to define content
- Understanding routing within Nuxt
- Building a Vue project with Server-Side Rendering
- Building a Vue project as a static site

Nuxt

Nuxt introduces the concept of Universal Vue Applications, as it allows us to take advantage of **Server-Side Rendering (SSR)** with ease. At the same time, Nuxt also gives us the ability to generate static sites, which means that the content is rendered as HTML, CSS, and JS files without going backward and forward from the server.

That's not all—Nuxt handles route generation and doesn't detract from any core features of Vue. Let's create a Nuxt project.

Creating a Nuxt project

We can use Vue CLI to create a new Nuxt project using the starter template. This provides us with a barebones Nuxt project and saves us from having to configure everything manually. We'll be creating a "recipe list" application named "Hearty Home Cooking" that uses a REST API to get category and recipe names. Run the following command in your Terminal to create a new Nuxt project:

```
# Create a new Nuxt project
$ vue init nuxt-community/starter-template vue-nuxt

# Change directory
$ cd vue-nuxt

# Install dependencies
$ npm install

# Run the project in the browser
$ npm run dev
```

The preceding steps are quite similar to what we've come to expect when creating a new Vue project, instead, we can simply use the Nuxt repository and starter template to generate a project.

If we take a look at our `package.json`, you'll see that we don't have a list of production dependencies; instead, we just have one, `nuxt`:

```
"dependencies": {
  "nuxt": "^1.0.0"
}
```

This is important, as this means we don't have to manage the version of Vue or worry about other compatible packages since we only need to update the version of `nuxt`.

Directory structure

If we open our project up inside the editor, we'll note that we have substantially more folders than our previous Vue applications. I've compiled a table that outlines what they mean:

Folder	Description
Assets	Used to store project assets, such as uncompiled images, js, and CSS. Uses Webpack loaders to load as modules.
Components	Used to store application components. These are not converted to routes.
Layouts	Used to create application layouts, such as default, error, or other custom layouts.
Middleware	Used to define custom application middleware. This allows us to run the custom functionality on different events, such as navigating between pages.
Pages	Used to create components (the .vue file) that serve as application routes.
Plugins	Used to register application-wide plugins (that is, with Vue.use).
Static	Used to store static files; each item inside this folder is mapped to /* instead of /static/*.
Store	Used with the Vuex store. Both the standard and module implementations of Vuex can be used with Nuxt.

Although this may seem more complex, keep in mind that this helps us separate our concerns, and the structure allows Nuxt to handle things such as autoroute generation.

Nuxt configuration

Let's add some custom links to our project so that we can take advantage of CSS libraries, fonts, and more. Let's add Bulma to our project.

Bulma is a CSS framework that allows us to build applications with Flexbox and lets us take advantage of many premade components. We can add it (and other external CDN files) to our project by navigating to nuxt.config.js and adding a new object to our link object within the head object, like so:

```
head: {
  // Omitted
  link: [
```

```
    { rel: 'icon', type: 'image/x-icon', href: '/favicon.ico' },
    {
      rel: 'stylesheet',
      href:
    'https://cdnjs.cloudflare.com/ajax/libs/bulma/0.6.1/css/bulma.min.css',
    },
  ],
}
```

If we then use the developer tools to check the head inside of our HTML document, you'll note that Bulma has been added to our project. If we head over to our developer tools we can see that it does indeed use Bulma within the project:

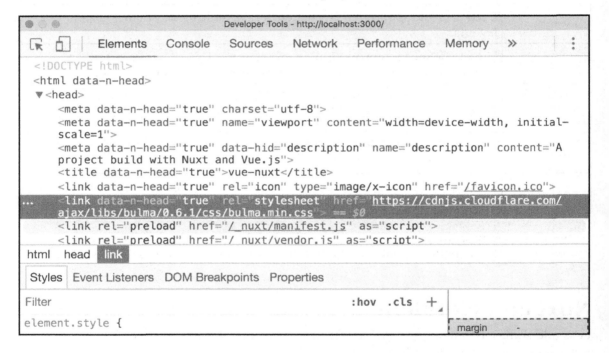

Navigation

Each time we create a new `.vue` file inside the pages directory, we're given a new route for our application. This means that any time we want to create a new route, we just create a new folder with the route name and the rest is handled by Nuxt. Given that we have default `index.vue` in our `pages` folder, the routes initially look like this:

```
routes: [
  {
    name: 'index',
    path: '/',
    component: 'pages/index.vue'
  }
]
```

If we then add a `categories` folder with an `index.vue` inside, Nuxt would generate the following routes:

```
routes: [
  {
    name: 'index',
    path: '/',
    component: 'pages/index.vue'
  },
  {
    name: 'categories',
    path: '/categories',
    component: 'pages/categories/index.vue'
  }
]
```

If we want to take advantage of dynamic route parameters, such as an `id`, we can make a component named `_id.vue` inside the `categories` folder. This automatically creates a route with the `id` parameter, allowing us to take action based on a user's selection:

```
routes: [
  {
    name: 'index',
    path: '/',
    component: 'pages/index.vue'
  },
  {
    name: 'categories',
    path: '/categories',
    component: 'pages/categories/index.vue'
  },
  {
    name: 'categories-id',
    path: '/categories/id',
    component: 'pages/categories/_id.vue'
  }
]
```

Navigating between routes

How do we navigate between routes with Nuxt? Well, we do so using the `nuxt-link` component, of course!

This is similar to the `router-link` component that's used when navigating between links with a standard Vue.js application (and as of writing, it is identical to it), but this is wrapped with the `nuxt-link` component to take advantage of features, such as prefetching, in the future.

Layouts

We can create custom layouts inside our Nuxt project. This allows us to change the way our pages are arranged and also allows us to add commonalities, such as static navigation bars and footers. Let's use Bulma to create a new navigation bar that allows us to navigate between multiple components within our site.

Inside the `components` folder, make a new file called `NavigationBar.vue` and give it the following markup:

```
<template>
  <nav class="navbar is-primary" role="navigation" aria-label="main
  navigation">
    <div class="navbar-brand">
      <nuxt-link class="navbar-item" to="/">Hearty Home Cooking</nuxt-
      link>
    </div>
  </nav>
</template>

<script>
export default {}
</script>
```

We then need to add this to our default layout inside `layouts/default.vue`. I've also enclosed the `nuxt` tag (that is, our main `router-view`) with appropriate Bulma classes to center our content:

```
<template>
  <div>
    <navigation-bar></navigation-bar>
    <section class="section">
      <nuxt class="container"/>
    </section>
```

```
    </div>
</template>

<script>
import NavigationBar from '../components/NavigationBar'

export default {
  components: {
    NavigationBar
  }
}
</script>
```

If we then head to the browser, we have an application that looks like this, reflecting our code:

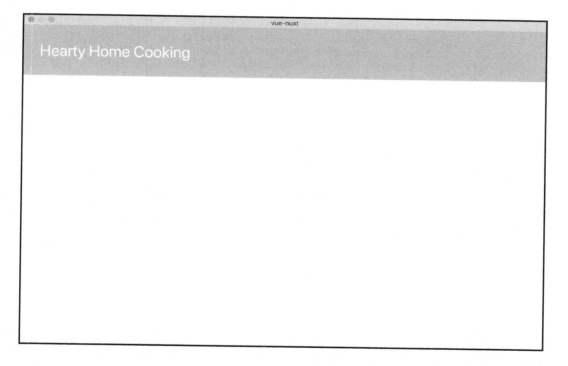

The Mock REST API

Before we create the components to display our data, let's mock out a REST API with JSON Server. To do this, we'll need a file named db.json inside the root of our project, as follows:

```
{
  "recipes": [
    { "id": 1, "title": "Blueberry and Chocolate Cake", "categoryId": 1,
"image": "https://static.pexels.com/photos/291528/pexels-photo-291528.jpeg"
},
    { "id": 2, "title": "Chocolate Cheesecake", "categoryId": 1, "image":
"https://images.pexels.com/photos/47013/pexels-photo-47013.jpeg"},
    { "id": 3, "title": "New York and Berry Cheesecake", "categoryId": 1,
"image": "https://images.pexels.com/photos/14107/pexels-photo-14107.jpeg"},
    { "id": 4, "title": "Salad with Light Dressing", "categoryId": 2,
"image":
"https://static.pexels.com/photos/257816/pexels-photo-257816.jpeg"},
    { "id": 5, "title": "Salmon Slices", "categoryId": 2, "image":
"https://static.pexels.com/photos/629093/pexels-photo-629093.jpeg" },
    { "id": 6, "title": "Mushroom, Tomato and Sweetcorn Pizza",
"categoryId": 3, "image":
"https://static.pexels.com/photos/7658/food-pizza-box-chalkboard.jpg" },
    { "id": 7, "title": "Fresh Burger", "categoryId": 4, "image":
"https://images.pexels.com/photos/460599/pexels-photo-460599.jpeg" }
  ],
  "categories": [
    { "id": 1, "name": "Dessert", "description": "Delcious desserts that
range from creamy New York style cheesecakes to scrumptious blueberry and
chocolate cakes."},
    { "id": 2, "name": "Healthy Eating", "description": "Healthy options
don't have to be boring with our fresh salmon slices and sweet, crispy
salad."},
    { "id": 3, "name": "Pizza", "description": "Pizza is always a popular
choice, chef up the perfect meat feast with our recipes!"},
    { "id": 4, "name": "Burgers", "description": "Be the king of the party
with our flagship BBQ Burger recipe, or make something lighter with our
veggie burgers!"}
  ]
}
```

Next, ensure that you have JSON Server installed on your machine by running the following command in the Terminal:

```
$ npm install json-server -g
```

We can then run the server on the 3001 port (or any port other than 3000 because this is what Nuxt runs on) by typing the following command in the Terminal:

```
$ json-server --watch db.json --port 3001
```

This will watch for any changes to our database and update the API accordingly. We'll then be able to make requests to localhost:3000/recipes/:id and localhost:3000/categories/:id. In Nuxt, we can do this with axios and asyncData; let's take a look at that next.

asyncData

We can use the asyncData method to resolve data for our component before the component is loaded, essentially requesting data on the server side and then merging the results with the data object inside our component instance when loaded. This makes it a great place to add asynchronous actions, such as getting data from a REST API.

We'll use the axios library to create HTTP requests, so we'll need to ensure that we've installed it. Run the following from your Terminal:

```
$ npm install axios
```

Then, inside pages/index.vue, we will get a list of categories to show the user when our application starts. Let's do that inside asyncData:

```
import axios from 'axios'

export default {
  asyncData ({ req, params }) {
    return axios.get(`http://localhost:3001/categories`)
      .then((res) => {
        return {
          categories: res.data
        }
      })
  },
}
```

Categories

As `asyncData` is merged with our Vue instance's data object, we can then access the data inside of our view. Let's create a `category` component that displays a category for each category inside our API:

```
<template>
  <div class="card">
    <header class="card-header">
      <p class="card-header-title">
        {{category.name}}
      </p>
    </header>
    <div class="card-content">
      <div class="content">
        {{category.description}}
      </div>
    </div>
    <footer class="card-footer">
      <nuxt-link :to="categoryLink" class="card-footer-
      item">View</nuxt-link>
    </footer>
  </div>
</template>

<script>

export default {
  props: ['category'],
  computed: {
    categoryLink () {
      return `/categories/${this.category.id}`
    }
  }
}
</script>

<style scoped>
div {
  margin: 10px;
}
</style>
```

In the preceding code, we used Bulma to take the category information and placed it on a card. We also used a `computed` property to generate the prop for the `nuxt-link` component. This allows us to navigate the user to a list of items based on category `id`. We can then add this to our root `pages/index.vue` file:

```
<template>
  <div>
    <app-category v-for="category in categories" :key="category.id"
     :category="category"></app-category>
  </div>
</template>

<script>
import Category from '../components/Category'
import axios from 'axios'

export default {
  asyncData ({ req, params }) {
    return axios.get(`http://localhost:3001/categories`)
      .then((res) => {
        return {
          categories: res.data
        }
      })
  },
  components: {
    'app-category': Category
  }
}
</script>
```

As a result, this is what our front page now looks like:

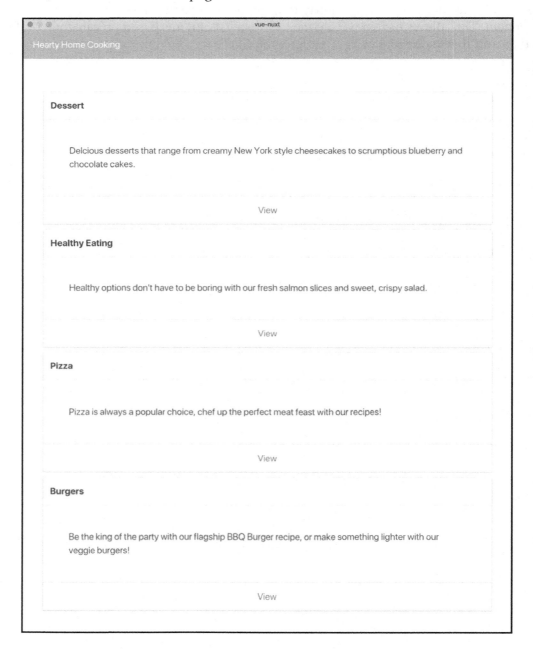

Category detail

In order to navigate the user to the `category` detail page, we'll need to create a `_id.vue` file inside the `categories` folder. This will give us access to the ID parameter inside this page. This process is similar to before, except that now we've also added a `validate` function that checks whether the `id` parameter exists:

```
<script>
import axios from 'axios'

export default {
  validate ({ params }) {
    return !isNaN(+params.id)
  },
  asyncData ({ req, params }) {
    return axios.get(`http://localhost:3001/recipes?
    categoryId=${params.id}`)
      .then((res) => {
        return {
          recipes: res.data
        }
      })
  },
}
</script>
```

The `validate` function ensures that the parameter exists for this route, and if it doesn't exist, it will navigate the user to an error (404) page. Later on in this chapter, we'll get the hang of how to create our own error pages.

We now have a `recipes` array inside our `data` object that contains recipes based on the `categoryId` that the user selected. Let's create a `Recipe.vue` component inside the components folder that displays recipe information:

```
<template>
  <div class="recipe">
    <div class="card">
      <div class="card-image">
        <figure class="image is-4by3">
          <img :src="recipe.image">
        </figure>
      </div>
      <div class="card-content has-text-centered">
        <div class="content">
          {{recipe.title}}
        </div>
```

```
        </div>
      </div>
    </div>
  </template>

<script>

export default {
  props: ['recipe']
}
</script>

<style>
.recipe {
  padding: 10px;
  margin: 5px;
}
</style>
```

Once again, we're using Bulma for styling and are able to pass a recipe into this component as a prop. Let's iterate over all recipes inside our _id.vue component:

```
<template>
  <div>
    <app-recipe v-for="recipe in recipes" :key="recipe.id"
    :recipe="recipe"></app-recipe>
  </div>
</template>

<script>
import Recipe from '../../components/Recipe'
import axios from 'axios'

export default {
  validate ({ params }) {
    return !isNaN(+params.id)
  },
  asyncData ({ req, params }) {
    return axios.get(`http://localhost:3001/recipes?
    categoryId=${params.id}`)
      .then((res) => {
        return {
          recipes: res.data
        }
      })
  },
  components: {
```

```
      'app-recipe': Recipe
    }
  }
</script>
```

Whenever we select a category, we now get the following page, which shows the selected recipes:

Error page

What if the user navigates to a route that doesn't exist or there's an error in our application? Well, we certainly could take advantage of Nuxt's default error page, or we could create our own.

We can do that by creating `error.vue` inside the `layouts` folder. Let's go ahead and do that and display an error message if the status code is `404`; if not, we'll display a generic error message:

```
<template>
  <div>
    <div class="has-text-centered" v-if="error.statusCode === 404">
      <img src="https://images.pexels.com/photos/127028/pexels-photo-
      127028.jpeg" alt="">
        <h1 class="title">Page not found: 404</h1>
        <h2 class="subtitle">
          <nuxt-link to="/">Back to the home page</nuxt-link>
        </h2>
    </div>
    <div v-else class="has-text-centered">
      <h1 class="title">An error occured.</h1>
      <h2 class="subtitle">
        <nuxt-link to="/">Back to the home page</nuxt-link>
      </h2>
    </div>
  </div>
</template>

<script>

export default {
  props: ['error'],
}
</script>
```

If we then navigate to `localhost:3000/e`, you'll be navigated to our error page. Let's take a look at the error page:

Plugins

We'll need the ability to add recipes to our application; as adding new recipes will require a form and some input(s) in order to appropriately validate the form, we'll use Vuelidate. If you remember from previous chapters, we can add Vuelidate and other plugins with Vue.use. The process is similar when using Nuxt, but requires an extra step. Let's install Vuelidate by running the following command in the Terminal:

```
$ npm install vuelidate
```

Inside our plugins folder, make a new file named Vuelidate.js. Inside this file, we can import Vue and Vuelidate and add the plugin:

```
import Vue from 'vue'
import Vuelidate from 'vuelidate'

Vue.use(Vuelidate)
```

We can then update nuxt.config.js to add the plugins array, which points toward our Vuelidate file:

```
plugins: ['~/plugins/Vuelidate']
```

Inside the build object, we'll also add 'vuelidate' to the vendor bundle so that it's added to our application:

```
build: {
 vendor: ['vuelidate'],
 // Omitted
}
```

Adding recipes

Let's make a new route under pages/Recipes/new.vue; this will then generate a route to localhost:3000/recipes/new. Our implementation will be simple; for example, having recipe steps as string may not be the best idea for production, but it allows us to achieve our goal(s) in development.

We can then add the appropriate data object and validation(s) with `Vuelidate`:

```
import { required, minLength } from 'vuelidate/lib/validators'

export default {
  data () {
    return {
      title: '',
      image: '',
      steps: '',
      categoryId: 1
    }
  },
  validations: {
    title: {
      required,
      minLength: minLength(4)
    },
    image: {
      required
    },
    steps: {
      required,
      minLength: minLength(30)
    }
  },
}
```

Next up, we can add the appropriate template, which includes everything from validation messages, to contextual classes, and enabling/disabling the `submit` button if the form is valid/invalid:

```
<template>
  <form @submit.prevent="submitRecipe">
    <div class="field">
      <label class="label">Recipe Title</label>
      <input class="input" :class="{ 'is-danger': $v.title.$error}" v-
      model.trim="title" @input="$v.title.$touch()" type="text">
      <p class="help is-danger" v-if="!$v.title.required &&
      $v.title.$dirty">Title is required</p>
      <p class="help is-danger" v-if="!$v.title.minLength &&
      $v.title.$dirty">Title must be at least 4 characters.</p>
    </div>

    <div class="field">
      <label class="label">Recipe Image URL</label>
      <input class="input" :class="{ 'is-danger': $v.image.$error}" v-
```

```
          model.trim="image" @input="$v.image.$touch()" type="text">
          <p class="help is-danger" v-if="!$v.image.required &&
          $v.image.$dirty">Image URL is required</p>
        </div>

        <div class="field">
          <label class="label">Steps</label>
          <textarea class="textarea" rows="5" :class="{ 'is-danger':
          $v.steps.$error}" v-model="steps" @input="$v.steps.$touch()"
          type="text">
          </textarea>
          <p class="help is-danger" v-if="!$v.steps.required &&
          $v.steps.$dirty">Recipe steps are required.</p>
          <p class="help is-danger" v-if="!$v.steps.minLength &&
          $v.steps.$dirty">Steps must be at least 30 characters.</p>
        </div>

        <div class="field">
          <label class="label">Category</label>
          <div class="control">
            <div class="select">
              <select v-model="categoryId" @input="$v.categoryId.$touch()">
                <option value="1">Dessert</option>
                <option value="2">Healthy Eating</option>
              </select>
            </div>
          </div>
        </div>

        <button :disabled="$v.$invalid" class="button is-
      primary">Add</button>
    </form>
</template>
```

To submit the recipe, we'll need to make a POST request to our API:

```
import axios from 'axios'

export default {
  // Omitted
  methods: {
    submitRecipe () {
      const recipe = { title: this.title, image: this.image, steps:
      this.steps, categoryId: Number(this.categoryId) }
      axios.post('http://localhost:3001/recipes', recipe)
    }
  },
}
```

Instead of navigating to the `http://localhost:3000/recipes/new` URL manually, let's add an item to our navigation bar:

```
<template>
  <nav class="navbar is-primary" role="navigation" aria-label="main
navigation">
    <div class="navbar-brand">
      <nuxt-link class="navbar-item" to="/">Hearty Home Cooking</nuxt-
      link>
    </div>
    <div class="navbar-end">
      <nuxt-link class="navbar-item" to="/recipes/new">+ Add New
      Recipe</nuxt-
      link>
    </div>
  </nav>
</template>
```

Here's what our page now looks like:

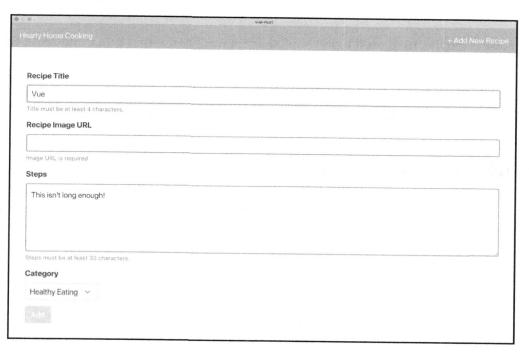

Although we haven't used the recipe steps in our application, I've included it in this example as a feature you may want to include yourself.

Transitions

When navigating between pages, Nuxt makes adding transitions super simple. Let's add a `transition` to each navigation action by adding custom CSS. Add a file named `transition.css` into the `assets` folder, and we'll hook into the various different page states:

```css
.page-enter-active, .page-leave-active {
  transition: all 0.25s;
}

.page-enter, .page-leave-active {
  opacity: 0;
  transform: scale(2);
}
```

After adding the file, we'll need to tell Nuxt that we want to use it as a `.css` file. Add the following code to your `nuxt.config.js`:

```
css: ['~/assets/transition.css']
```

Now, we can navigate between any page and we'll have a page transition each time.

Building for production

Nuxt offers us a variety of ways to build our project for production, such as server-rendered (Universal), static, or **Single Page Application (SPA)** mode. All of these offer different pros and cons, depending on the use case.

By default, our project is in server-rendered (Universal) mode and can be built for production by running the following command in the Terminal:

```
$ npm run build
```

We then get a `dist` folder inside the `.nuxt` folder within our project; this contains the built end result(s) of our application, which can be deployed to a hosting provider:

```
● ● ●                         Shell                          Shell

DONE  Compiled successfully in 6074ms                          2:48:38 AM

Hash: 16c7ec03b54c8892d95e
Version: webpack 3.10.0
Time: 6074ms
                                  Asset      Size  Chunks                 Chunk Names
       pages/Recipes/new.85c2bcb26a5a4d92d073.js   23.2 kB       0  [emitted]  pages/Recipes/new
            pages/index.d2736d8007be480945d3.js   14.7 kB       1  [emitted]  pages/index
   pages/Categories/_id.14ba3fc40aa6fde8ed35.js   14.3 kB       2  [emitted]  pages/Categories/_id
       layouts/default.ede1e407e90c33249804.js   1.34 kB       3  [emitted]  layouts/default
     pages/Recipes/_id.d7f3f217eff87872307c.js  210 bytes       4  [emitted]  pages/Recipes/_id
             vendor.7249ad82eda605563117.js    161 kB       5  [emitted]  vendor
                 app.d66851dfec61c45a8b84.js   27.8 kB       6  [emitted]  app
             manifest.16c7ec03b54c8892d95e.js   1.68 kB       7  [emitted]  manifest
                               LICENSES   1.01 kB          [emitted]
  + 3 hidden assets
Hash: 539a9808580be4c52c51
Version: webpack 3.10.0
Time: 382ms
             Asset    Size  Chunks              Chunk Names
server-bundle.json   151 kB          [emitted]
  nuxt:build Building done +7s
Pauls-iMac:vue-nuxt paulhalliday$
```

Static

In order to build our project in static mode, we can run the following command in the Terminal:

```
$ npm run generate
```

This will build a static site, which can then be deployed to a static hosting provider such as Firebase. This is how the Terminal should appear:

```
Time: 6345ms
                                    Asset     Size  Chunks                   Chunk Names
       pages/Recipes/new.85c2bcb26a5a4d92d073.js   23.2 kB       0  [emitted]  pages/Recipes/new
              pages/index.d2736d8007be480945d3.js   14.7 kB       1  [emitted]  pages/index
     pages/Categories/_id.14ba3fc40aa6fde8ed35.js   14.3 kB       2  [emitted]  pages/Categories/_id
         layouts/default.ede1e407e90c33249804.js   1.34 kB       3  [emitted]  layouts/default
      pages/Recipes/_id.d7f3f217eff87872307c.js  210 bytes       4  [emitted]  pages/Recipes/_id
                    vendor.7249ad82eda605563117.js    161 kB       5  [emitted]  vendor
                       app.48a2f8d4afe190d642aa.js   28.1 kB       6  [emitted]  app
                 manifest.40adb286bcb4fc0982b4.js   1.68 kB       7  [emitted]  manifest
                                          LICENSES   1.01 kB          [emitted]
 + 2 hidden assets
  nuxt: Call generate:distRemoved hooks (1) +0ms
  nuxt:generate Destination folder cleaned +7s
  nuxt: Call generate:distCopied hooks (1) +23ms
  nuxt:generate Static & build files copied +23ms
  nuxt:render Rendering url / +0ms
  nuxt:render Rendering url /Recipes/new +2ms
  nuxt: Call generate:page hooks (1) +45ms
  nuxt: Call generate:page hooks (1) +3ms
  nuxt:generate Generate file: /index.html +48ms
  nuxt:generate Generate file: /Recipes/new/index.html +0ms
  nuxt: Call generate:done hooks (1) +89ms
  nuxt:generate HTML Files generated in 6.9s +90ms
  nuxt:generate Generate done +0ms
Pauls-iMac:vue-nuxt paulhalliday$
```

SPA mode

To build our project in the SPA mode, we will need to add the following key value to `nuxt.config.js`:

```
mode: 'spa'
```

We can then build our project once again, but this time it'll be built using SPA mode:

```
$ npm run build
```

Our command Terminal should now look like the following:

```
● ● ●                    Shell                              Shell
Time: 6025ms
                                  Asset       Size  Chunks              Chunk Names
      pages/Recipes/new.85c2bcb26a5a4d92d073.js  23.2 kB      0  [emitted]  pages/Recipes/new
            pages/index.d2736d8007be480945d3.js  14.7 kB      1  [emitted]  pages/index
    pages/Categories/_id.14ba3fc40aa6fde8ed35.js  14.3 kB      2  [emitted]  pages/Categories/_id
        layouts/default.ede1e407e90c33249804.js  1.34 kB      3  [emitted]  layouts/default
      pages/Recipes/_id.d7f3f217eff87872307c.js  210 bytes    4  [emitted]  pages/Recipes/_id
              vendor.7249ad82eda605563117.js  161 kB      5  [emitted]  vendor
              app.48a2f8d4afe190d642aa.js  28.1 kB      6  [emitted]  app
          manifest.40adb286bcb4fc0982b4.js  1.68 kB      7  [emitted]  manifest
                              LICENSES  1.01 kB         [emitted]
+ 2 hidden assets
  nuxt: Call generate:distRemoved hooks (1) +0ms
  nuxt:build Destination folder cleaned +6s
  nuxt: Call generate:distCopied hooks (1) +36ms
  nuxt:build Static & build files copied +37ms
  nuxt:render Rendering url / +0ms
  nuxt:render Rendering url /Recipes/new +3ms
  nuxt: Call generate:page hooks (1) +9ms
  nuxt: Call generate:page hooks (1) +1ms
  nuxt:build Generate file: /index.html +9ms
  nuxt:build Generate file: /Recipes/new/index.html +0ms
  nuxt: Call generate:done hooks (1) +1ms
  nuxt:build HTML Files generated in 6.5s +1ms
✓ You can now directly upload dist/ or start server using "nuxt start"
Pauls-iMac:vue-nuxt paulhalliday$ 
```

Summary

In this chapter, we discussed how to use Nuxt to create server-rendered Vue applications. We also discussed just *how easy* it is to create new routes and how to add custom CSS libraries inside our project. Furthermore, we covered how we can add transitions to our pages to make it interesting when switching between routes. We also covered how we can build different versions of our project, depending on whether we want a universal, static, or SPA application.

In the final chapter, we'll be discussing common anti-patterns within Vue.js and how to avoid them. This is paramount to writing consistent software that can survive the test of time.

13
Patterns

In this chapter, we'll look at a variety of anti-patterns within Vue.js and review concepts at a high level that we've learned throughout the book. We'll look at various patterns and anti-patterns and how we can write code that is consistent across teams and your own projects.

Before defining anything as a *pattern* or *anti-pattern*, it's important to accurately define both for the reader. If something is to be considered a pattern, this means that this is a recommended practice in the vast majority of cases. On the contrary, if I've defined it as an anti-pattern, then it's most likely not a recommended practice in a vast majority of cases. For further information on this, a good source of patterns and guidelines can be found at https://github.com/pablohpsilva/vuejs-component-style-guide.

Software development is an opinionated field with a variety of ways to solve the same problem, so there may be ideologies that are classified as something you don't agree with, and that's okay. At the end of the day, each team has their own style, but developers should seek to stick to patterns that reduce friction and speed up development where possible.

In this chapter, we'll learn about the following topics:

- Common patterns and anti-patterns within Vue projects
- Container/presentational components
- How to write testable Vue.js components

Components

There are many ways for components to communicate within Vue, such as the use of props, events, and store-based scenarios. Vue also gives us access to $parent and $children objects, which allow us to interact with parent/child components. Let's take a look at this and see why it shouldn't be used.

Communication – Anti-pattern

Imagine that we had our familiar TodoList example, and within the TodoItem component, we want the ability to complete a particular Todo. If we wanted to keep our todos within the TodoList and thus call the completed method from TodoItem, we could do it like this:

```
export default {
  props: ['todo'],
  methods: {
    completeTodo(todo) {
      this.$parent.$options.methods.completeTodo(todo);
    }
  }
}
```

This is a bad idea for numerous reasons, mostly because we're tightly coupling these two components together and assuming that there will always be a completeTodo method on the parent component.

What can we change about this to make it better?

I'm not saying that parent/child components can't communicate, but you should aim to design components in such a way that they're flexible. Use events or the Vuex store depending on the structure of your application. Here's an example using an event instead:

```
methods: {
  completeTodo(todo) {
    this.$emit('completeTodo', todo)
  }
}
```

Children mutating props – Anti-pattern

It's important that we won't modify props inside our child components. Props should be considered the source of truth when passed down to a component and thus, change the value from within a child component is typically bad practice. There are some unique case scenarios however where it may be appropriate to do so, like when using the `.sync` modifier to achieve two-way data binding.

If we use our previous example and change the todos prop from within the child, we'll get a warning inside the console:

```
methods: {
  completeTodo(todo) {
    this.todo = [{id: 1, name: 'Do the dishes.'}];
    this.$emit('completeTodo', todo)
  }
}
```

What should we do instead?

If you want to work with the prop inside the child component, it's best to save the prop as a new variable inside the `data` option. This allows you to then mutate a new version of the prop, local to this component:

```
export default {
  props: {
    age: {
      type: Number,
    }
  },
  data() {
    return {
      personAge: this.age
    }
  },
}
```

We can then access and mutate `personAge` without worrying about any side effects. Another example can be seen when creating a filterable search box, where instead of mutating the prop directly, make a `computed` property that performs the required functions:

```
export default {
  props: {
```

```
      filter: {
        type: String,
      }
    },
    computed: {
      trimFilter() {
        return this.filter.trim().toLowerCase()
      }
    }
  }
```

Mutating property arrays

An important consideration to make when passing down arrays and objects as properties within JavaScript is the fact that they are passed by reference. This means that any changes to the original array within the child will also spill over into the parent component. Let's see this in action:

```
<template>
  <div>
    <h1>Parent Component</h1>
    <ul>
      <li v-for="friend in friendList"
:key="friend.id">{{friend.name}}</li>
    </ul>

    <Person :friendList="friendList" />
  </div>
</template>

<script>
import Person from './components/Person';

export default {
  data() {
    return {
      friendList: [{ id: 1, name: 'John Doe' }]
    }
  },
  components: {
    Person
  }
}
</script>
```

Here, we have a component (App.vue) that contains an array that we're displaying on screen and passing down into the child component. We'll display the same array on screen inside the child component, but also give the child a button to add a new item into the array:

```
<template>
  <div>
    <h1>Child Component</h1>
    <ul>
      <li v-for="friend in friendList"
:key="friend.id">{{friend.name}}</li>
    </ul>
    <button @click="addFriend">Add Friend</button>
  </div>
</template>

<script>
export default {
  props: {
    friendList: {
      type: Array,
    }
  },
  methods: {
    addFriend() {
      this.friendList.push({ id: 2, name: 'Sarah Doe' })
    }
  }
}
</script>
```

When we add a new person to our friends' list, this is our result:

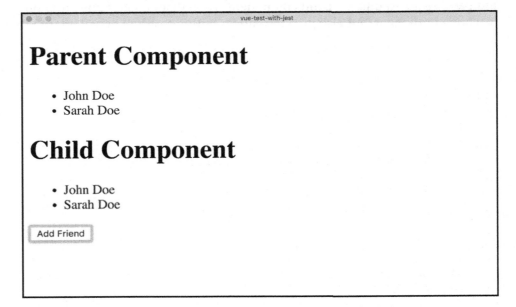

Then, both components have the same array! This isn't what we want. If for some reason we wanted to do an action like this, it would be wiser to keep a copy of the friends' list and mutate that, as follows:

```
export default {
  props: {
    friendList: {
      type: Array,
    }
  },
  data() {
    return {
      fList: [...this.friendList]
    }
  },
  methods: {
    addFriend() {
      this.fList.push({ id: 2, name: 'Sarah Doe' })
    }
  }
}
```

Using data as an object - Anti-Pattern

When creating components with Vue, it's important that the data option is a function that returns a new object holding data, rather than just a plain data object.

If you simply use a data object that's not a function, all instances of the component will share the same data. This is bad because as you may be able to imagine, all instances of the component will be updated with the same data any time it changes. It's important to ensure that each component is capable of managing its own data rather than sharing data across the board.

Let's take a look at the problem:

```
data: {
  recipeList: [],
  selectedCategory: 'Desserts'
}
```

We can fix this by doing this instead:

```
data () {
  return {
    recipeList: [],
    selectedCategory: 'Desserts'
  }
}
```

By creating the `return` statement, it allows each instance created to have its own object rather than a shared one. This then allows the code to be used multiple times without the conflict of shared data.

Next up, let's take a look at best practices for naming our components.

Naming components – Anti-pattern

It's not a good idea to name components in single words as it has the chance to conflict with native HTML elements. Let's say we had a signup form and a component named `Form.vue`; what would be an appropriate name when using this inside our template?

Well, as you might imagine, having a component named `<form>` will conflict with the `<form>`, so it's a best practice to have components that are named with more than one word. A better example can be the name of `signup-form`, `app-signup-form`, or `app-form`, depending on preference:

```
// This would not be an appropriate name as it conflicts with HTML
elements.
Vue.component('form', Form)

// This is a better name as it's multi-word and there are less chances to
conflict.
Vue.component('signup-form', Form)
```

Template expressions

Often times, when we're displaying items on the screen, we may have to compute values and call functions to change the way our data looks. Instead of doing this work inside the template, it's advised to move this out into a `computed` property, as this is much easier to maintain:

```
// Bad
<nuxt-link :to="`/categories/${this.category.id}`" class="card-footer-
item">View</nuxt-link>

// Good
<nuxt-link :to="categoryLink" class="card-footer-item">View</nuxt-link>

export default {
  props: ['category'],
  computed: {
    categoryLink () {
      return `/categories/${this.category.id}`
    }
  }
}
```

This means any changes in our template are much easier to handle because the output is mapped to a computed property.

Pattern – Container/Presentational components

An important part of the component design is ensuring that your components are testable. You should think of each component as a standalone module in your application that could be switched in/out, as necessary; as a result, it should not be tightly coupled with another component.

The best way is to ensure that your components are testable after ensuring that light coupling is to have a well-defined public API via component props and then use events to communicate between the parent/child component. This also helps us when testing, as we're able to mock components much easier.

A common pattern to use when following this model is the container/presentational components. This means we keep all of our business logic and state inside the "container" and then pass the state down to the "presentational" component to display on the screen.

The presentational component can still communicate with other components, if necessary, with the use of events, but it shouldn't modify or hold state outside inbound props. This ensures that we have a common data flow between our components, and it means that our applications are easier to reason about.

Here's an explicitly named component—DogContainer.vue:

```
<template>
  <dog-presentational :dogName="dogName" @woof="woof"></dog-presentational>
</template>

<script>
import DogPresentational from './DogPresentational'

export default {
  data() {
    return {
      dogName: 'Coco',
    }
  },
  components: {
    'dog-presentational': DogPresentational
  },
  methods: {
    woof() {
```

```
        alert('Woof!');
      }
    },
  }
</script>
```

The container component has handed down the dog's name (and any other items) as a property into the presentational component. The container component is also listening for an event named `woof` on this component and is taking action by calling the `woof` method when it has been emitted. Here's our presentational component:

```
<template>
  <div>
    <h1>Name: {{dogName}}</h1>
    <button @click="woof">Woof</button>
  </div>
</template>

<script>
export default {
  props: ['dogName'],
  methods: {
    woof() {
      this.$emit('woof')
    }
  }
}
</script>
```

Our component's concerns are now clearly separated, and we have a clear communication path between them.

This composition can be visualized in the following figure:

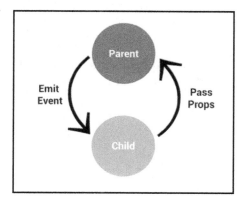

Composing components

Prop validation

While we should seek to communicate between child components via props, it's important to be verbose when validating properties by considering types, requirements, defaults, and so on. Throughout the book, I've used a mix of both techniques for brevity, but in production, props should be appropriately validated. Let's start out by looking at some examples of property types:

```
export default {
  props: {
    firstName: {
      type: String
    },
    lastName: {
      type: String
    },
    age: {
      type: Number
    },
    friendList: {
      type: Array
    }
  },
}
```

We also have various other types available such as Boolean, function, or any other constructor function (that is, type of Person). By accurately defining the types we expect, this allows us (and our team) to reason better about what we can expect within this component.

At the same time, we can also ensure that props are required. This should be done where necessary, allowing us to ensure that whenever the component is used, no required props are missing:

```
props: {
  firstName: {
    type: String,
    required: true,
    default: 'John'
  },
  lastName: {
    type: String,
    required: true,
    default: 'Doe'
  }
}
```

We should always seek to give our props default values where possible, as this reduces necessary configurations but still allows the component to be customized if a developer wants. When dealing with objects and arrays, a function is used as a default parameter to avoid issues where instances share the same value.

```
props: {
  firstName: {
    type: String,
    default: 'John'
  },
  lastName: {
    type: String,
    default: 'Doe'
  },
  friendList: {
    type: Array,
    default: () => [{ id: 1, name: 'Paul Halliday'}]
  }
}
```

We can also assign a custom `validator` function for our properties. Let's say that we have a slot `machine` component that is only rendered if the user is `18` years or older:

```
props: {
  age: {
    type: Number,
    required: true,
    validator: value => {
      return value >= 18
    }
  },
}
```

Understanding reactivity

We've discussed reactivity and how it can be used in the previous chapters, but it's important to reconsider. When we're creating reactive data objects within Vue, it takes each property and adds appropriate getters/setters using `Object.defineProperty`. This allows Vue to handle changes to the object and notifies watchers, subsequently updating the component `https://vuejs.org/v2/guide/reactivity.html`. This can be visualized like so:

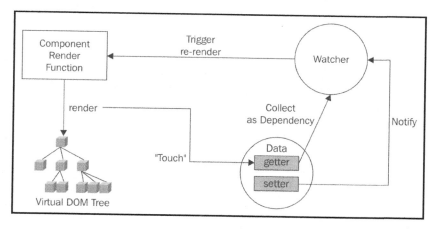

Visualizing Reactivity

This means that any property defined in the data option is automatically reactive. Here's an example:

```
export default {
  data() {
    return {
      name: 'Vue.js'
    }
  }
}
```

The name property is reactive inside this Vue instance, but if we were to add another property outside of the Vue instance, this would not be reactive. Let's take a look at an example:

```
export default {
  data() {
    return {
      items: [
        { id: 1, name: 'Bananas'},
        { id: 2, name: 'Pizza', quantity: 2},
        { id: 3, name: 'Cheesecake', quantity: 5}
      ]
    }
  },
}
```

Our groceries component has an items array that contains various objects. Every object has a quantity apart from the Bananas object, but we'd like to set the quantity for this. When using v-for it's important to include v-bind:key (or the shorthand :key) as it acts as a unique identifier for each item and by doing so allows for reuse and reordering of each node. Whilst key may be an attribute for v-for keep in mind it does have other use case scenarios.

```
<template>
  <div>
    <ul>
      <li v-for="(item, index) in items" :key="item.id"
@click="addQuantity(index)">
        {{item.name}} {{item.quantity}}
      </li>
    </ul>
  </div>
</template>

<script>
```

```
export default {
  data() {
    return {
      items: [
        { id: 1, name: 'Bananas'},
        { id: 2, name: 'Pizza', quantity: 2},
        { id: 3, name: 'Cheesecake', quantity: 5}
      ]
    }
  },
  methods: {
    addQuantity(selected) {
      this.items[selected].quantity = 1;
      console.log(this.items);
    }
  }
}
```

If we then head over to our browser, and proceed to use the dev tools to access the console we can see that the quantity has been set to hold a value for our object.

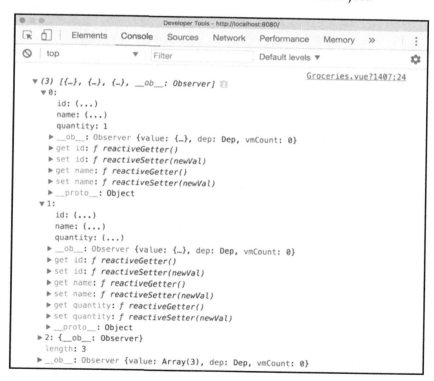

Note how there are reactive getters and setters for the quantity objects that contain quantity when defined inside the data object. Adding a property to the items after the fact means Vue doesn't add the appropriate getters/setters. If we wanted to do this, we'd have to use `Vue.set` instead:

```
methods: {
  addQuantity(selected) {
    const selectedItem = this.items[selected];
    this.$set(selectedItem, 'quantity', 2)
    console.log(this.items);
  }
}
```

This time, there are getters/setters for every property inside our instance:

Summary

In this chapter we looked at anti-patterns and patterns, and we have expanded our knowledge as to not only what they are, but also when it is appropriate to use them to coincide with best practices. Not only that, we also reviewed a lot of the concepts that we learned throughout the book in this chapter, along with considering some new ideas and techniques of what can be used going forward.

Reflecting on the previous chapters, we can look back and see how much ground we've covered. Practicing the techniques covered in this book will allow you to create scalable applications with Vue.js and build on what you've learned. Another important thing to remember is that **web development is always evolving**, the amount of *practical applications* for Vue continues to grow and *so should you*.

What next? Try new things! Build new projects, attend Vue.js meetings and conferences - find new ways of applying your skills to teach others. Not only will you have a positive impact on others, but you'll reaffirm your skills as a developer.

Other Books You May Enjoy

If you enjoyed this book, you may be interested in these other books by Packt:

Full-Stack Vue.js 2 and Laravel 5
Anthony Gore

ISBN: 978-1-78829-958-9

- Core features of Vue.js to create sophisticated user interfaces
- Build a secure backend API with Laravel
- Learn a state-of-the-art web development workflow with Webpack
- Full-stack app design principles and best practices
- Learn to deploy a full-stack app to a cloud server and CDN
- Managing complex application state with Vuex
- Securing a web service with Laravel Passport

Vue.js 2.x by Example
Mike Street

ISBN: 978-1-78829-346-4

- Looping through data with Vue.js
- Searching and filtering data
- Using components to display data
- Getting a list of files using the dropbox API
- Navigating through a file tree and loading folders from a URL
- Caching with Vuex
- Pre-caching for faster navigation
- Introducing vue-router and loading components
- Using vue-router dynamic routes to load data
- Using vue-router and Vuex to create an ecommerce store

Leave a review - let other readers know what you think

Please share your thoughts on this book with others by leaving a review on the site that you bought it from. If you purchased the book from Amazon, please leave us an honest review of this book's Amazon page. This is vital so that other potential readers can see and use your unbiased opinion to make purchasing decisions, we can understand what our customers think about our products, and our authors can see your feedback on the title that they have worked with Packt to create. It will only take a few minutes of your time but is valuable to other potential customers, our authors, and Packt. Thank you!

Index

Made in the USA
Middletown, DE
26 August 2019